Shopping Ad

How I Lived Beyond My Means in Order to

Become Someone Else

Sarah E. Jess

2017

Table of Contents

Introduction

I made the decision to write this book because finally, after more than two decades of struggling with a shopping addiction, I am relieved and grateful to realize that I am approaching the final stages towards healing. This superficial addiction is unfortunately prevalent in our society, especially among females, but does not often seem to be taken very seriously. I have found through my own experiences and long-term attempts to heal that there is a lack of resources and professional support available. It is my sincere hope that by sharing my personal account of my battle with shopping addiction, which ended up being intertwined with my great quest for a career, I may be an encouragement in the lives of others who are not sure where to turn or how to have hope for the future. Taking my addiction seriously and realizing that I had an actual problem was the first step to healing. This is my attempt to take a powerful negative from my life and to use it for good, helping others by shining a light on the path that brought me so much closer to freedom.

Chapter 1: Unsuspecting and Unaware

I can look back into my life at the age of twelve or thirteen, to discover the first stages of my shopping addiction just starting to develop. If I look back even further, I notice that one of my key weaknesses, greed, played a large role in my obsession with shopping. As a child I was a perfectionist when it came to material things. My room had to look perfect and clean, with everything in its place in order for me to feel at ease. I had dolls and toys, but spent more time enhancing their appearance than I did playing with them. I persuaded, bribed, and negotiated with my sisters in order to obtain the absolute best wardrobe for my Barbies. It was also in these early years that I became obsessed with money --- stealing loose change from my dad's dresser, going so far as to start a "bank" among my sisters with accounts for each of our four cats, and creating cash for my Barbies out of paper and foil. Of course, when this "bank" I had created eventually closed due to growing lack of participation by my sisters, I kept all of the money for myself. There was something about the challenge and the power that money brought that lured me, along with its ability to provide me with the best of the best of whatever I wanted.

I don't recall that my family went shopping very often when I was young, but whenever a back-to-school shopping trip was planned, or a trip to an out-of-town mall during spring or Christmas breaks was suggested by my mom, I became absolutely obsessed, thinking of and looking forward to nothing else. The allure of eating out and escaping the drudgery of everyday life, I am sure, played its role in my extreme excitement, but the thrill of spending money was like nothing I had ever experienced.

In the days before I became interested in clothing, my childish purchases consisted of gum, candy, lip-gloss,

2

stickers, and colorful pencils and markers decorated with cute characters. Even though there was no way I would ever be able to use all of the makers and pens myself, and I was in the habit of hoarding candy and gum until it went bad, I could never have enough. The colors, the scents, the variety … it was the adventure and the challenge of finding some new material things to add to my collections. Stickers I could earn by doing chores around the house, but my intense cravings for *MORE* seemed to surpass those of my sisters. I had so much more ambition than they had, fed by a whirlwind of greed.

As I hit my early teenage years, the amounts of money that I took from family members gradually increased. Before one of the much-anticipated shopping trips occurred, it was not uncommon for me to take a few twenties from whoever seemed to have a surplus. Guilt never touched me, and while I grew more attached to spending larger amounts of money than someone my age would normally have, my obedient sisters learned to build their savings accounts. It never occurred to them to spend very much, let alone to steal from the parents who provided for us. Just as it seldom occurred to me to save, unless I was prompted to do so by my mom.

My sisters and I grew up closely acquainted with addiction, and were extremely aware of the hereditary alcoholism our dad suffered from. Always cautious about the likelihood of one of us developing an alcohol addiction, shopping addiction quietly crept up on me, and secured an iron grip, before I ever had a chance to protest. It is obvious to me now when I look back, that the tiny seedling of a shopping addiction had planted itself inside of me when I was just a child. Should my conscience have instinctively prevented my addiction from growing? I seemed to be born too greedy to care.

I entered junior high school, and, like most other girls my age, I began to take an interest in fashion. The much bigger picture was my overall appearance. Clothing, unfortunately, was a great deal more expensive than the stickers and colorful pens I had left behind in elementary school. I certainly couldn't rely on my small allowance or the money I earned from cleaning my dad's hair salon to buy the things I was discovering that I needed. I became a teenager during the era of Guess jeans, Esprit, colored Keds, and Liz Claiborne purses. I got my first taste of Esprit clothing from our local department store; a white t-shirt with the Esprit logo screen printed in pastel lettering. I can still remember the smell of the store and of the shirt, and the way my heart raced as I paid $24 for this trendy addition to my wardrobe. I was both astonished and delighted by the compliments and acceptance I gained as a result of wearing my first logo t-shirt. I even saved the cardboard logo tag from the shirt, and taped it to one of the closet doors in my bedroom. I was hooked!! Fascinated, I would proudly stare at this logo, and dream of the next time when I could add another label to my door.

As everybody knows, the halls of a junior high school are brimming with fierce competition. The confident girls surrounding me had brown leather Eastland shoes with knotted laces, white Keds (some with the all-important Keds tag glued back in place), and stonewashed jeans pegged at the ankles. Fortunate and coincidentally more popular girls had Guess and Esprit sweatshirts, multiple Swatch watches, and Liz Claiborne purses to go with every outfit. Now, as a very introverted girl with untrendy red hair, I had never fit in, but had always stood out. These clothes, I knew, were the key to my acceptance. I wasn't so concerned about being noticed as I was with being left alone. Years of being teased and bullied had taken their toll. The more perfect and well-dressed I was, the greater chance I had of being respected and

6

untouchable. Popular girls who had never spoken to me before now went out of their way to comment about what I wore. And many of the bullies who had tormented me for years moved on to new unfashionable victims.

The first compliments I remember receiving in school were for wearing items of clothing that fit into the current trends. I quickly noticed that even adults treated you differently when you dressed in more expensive clothing. Again, my goal was never to become a part of the popular crowd with these clothes. Rather, I wanted to disassociate myself from the group of tormented misfits who floated through the hallways like frightened rabbits. As my wardrobe improved one piece at a time, respect from fellow students seemed to grow. I was able to choose and manipulate my own identity through what I wore, rather than being appointed one. People were kinder, and by becoming more aloof, I was able to escape the role of the teased and taunted one, and could indulge my quiet, creative side.

Chapter 2: Becoming Someone Else

By the time I entered high school, my creative side had found a major outlet. My hunger for shopping grew, and I discovered the thrill of hunting for unique items at thrift stores. My wardrobe in high school became quite a bit more costume-y. Vintage hats and coats, and wearing clothes wrong-side-out was my specialty. Each day's challenge was to create a new outfit. I bought new items of clothing whenever I could. A new larger mall had been built in our city, Piqua, and my family's first brief visit there was a trip to paradise. I can still recall the new mall smell, and a colorful accessories store called "The Canary and the Elephant". My undying wish was to go to the mall, and I constantly obsessed over when my next shopping trip would be.

My thirst for brand names was impossible to quench, so thank goodness I lived in a small city before the internet was around. By my second year of high school, and motivated by sheer determination, both of my closet doors were covered from top to bottom with logo labels from my purchases. Oh, the disappointment and low self-esteem that resulted from wearing the same outfit twice!! My sisters and I did not wear the same size, but I could still manage to create a new outfit for myself by borrowing items from their closets. More importantly, every day was a new fashion adventure. By creating a new look for tomorrow, I could escape the reality of today. Addiction alert! By controlling my image, I somewhat controlled how people perceived me, without saying a word. Fellow students who had never taken notice of me during junior high school or the early years of high school were suddenly interested in what I was wearing. I was no longer just the quiet daughter of a successful hair salon owner, and my red hair no longer seemed to precede me. Other previously hidden parts of my personality were now on display, creating a much desired distraction from my private self. In order to allow for these newly revealed sides of myself to dominate, and to keep them separate from my authentic and off-limits self, I began to assign myself different names. Some of the first ones I chose were Lavender Olivier, Francesca, and Isabella – whichever suited how I was feeling at the time, the fashion statement I hoped to make, and the colors and jewelry I favored at that point in time. I asked my friends to call me by the current name, and went so far as to introduce myself to new acquaintances using these names.

I grew easily bored, and so all of this creation became an exciting game! The thrill of taking cash from the alcoholic father I hated had the added benefit of giving me the ability to shop. Obtaining my driver's license allowed for more frequent trips to the mall and to thrift stores. A wad of cash and an entire shopping center full of stores for me to explore. Jewelry, handbags, shoes, pretty bras and panties, in addition to shirts, pants, skirts, and dresses in

11

endless color and fabric combinations…. I flitted back and forth between several groups of friends, never getting too close to anyone. No one else shared my love of fashion, and none of them could keep my attention for long. My true friend was shopping!

For an introverted and bored girl, a shopping mall equaled acceptance as well as entertainment. Sales associates were incredibly friendly to anyone with money to spend, and I remember feeling flattered, not wanting to let them down by not making a purchase. I discovered makeup and perfume, and everything else that my heart desired to transform me into whoever I felt like becoming next! Shopping elevated my mood and became associates with all positive feelings.

The summer before college was spent mainly with my new boyfriend. I was known as Francesca. Looking back, I am reminded that neither my first boyfriend nor his friends had money of their own. I suppose they were part of the entertainment I paid for. I worked eagerly at an Arby's restaurant; my first job outside of the family business. While I continued to clean my dad's hair salon on Sundays, I also boldly increased the amount of money I stole from my parents. My busier social life proved to be expensive. Very few of my earnings made their way into a savings account, as I was too involved in the present to be concerned about the future.

My boyfriend, his friends, and I frequently travelled to other nearby cities to eat and shop. His friends, I suppose, were really not my friends at all. I enjoyed the company, as well as a boyfriend who seemed as eager to shop as I was. I loved to spoil him with clothes, shoes, cologne, and anything else he told me that his poor upbringing had deprived him of. He was extremely handsome, and I needed him to be as well-dressed as I was. Appearance was everything! It wasn't too long, though, before I began

13

to feel used. Everything in our immature relationship seemed to depend on my purchasing power. The more arguments we had, the more I needed to shop just to feel better. And the more unsettling home life became when my angry alcoholic father was around, the more material things I seemed to need in order to dull the pain. Still, I had no idea what I was getting into. There was an obvious build-up of dangerous emotions inside of me. It felt like I would either break down or explode, and whatever it actually was, it was completely taking over me. I felt so lost, but in an unfair way, like someone had purposely misled me and then laughed about it. I really didn't know what to do, and so I shopped.

It was during these turbulent times in my life that I began ordering items from catalogues. Victoria's Secret and J. Crew were favorites, as was Design Toscano, where I could order fascinating antique reproductions and gargoyles to decorate my dorm room. Since online

14

shopping was not yet popular, ordering from catalogues opened up shopping possibilities all over the United States. And nothing compared to the excitement of receiving a package in the mail on an otherwise dreary and ordinary day. I especially loved the package when it was addressed to the name of the moment I was using. I believe my friends called me Kitty during this time, which stemmed I guess from my love of cats. I didn't realize it, but I was becoming less and less able to tolerate an average day, and relied more and more heavily on the twinge of excitement that shopping provided. The name "Sarah", my real name, brought to mind the pain of everyday life that Kitty and Francesca were easily able to escape.

Upon starting college, I took on a new part-time job at a local department store. It worked perfectly with my class schedule while I attended a community college, and then equally well on holidays and weekends when I transferred to my four year school located just an hour away from

15

home. I was elated to have an employee discount, and couldn't have been happier to spend so much time at the mall. While my sisters and friends worked at restaurants, gas stations, and or on campus, I felt privileged to dress up for work, and to be surrounded by an ever-changing inventory of clothing. Working in the junior's department, just across from cosmetics and beside the shoe department, there were temptations galore. Every day was an opportunity for a purchase, a new discovery, and, of course, to put items on hold for pay day. One way or another, I bought everything that I wanted. How could I resist, when I kept such a close eye on each item, knowing that if I didn't buy it today, the next customer could very well buy the last one in my size?

It never occurred to me to stop shopping. It never occurred to me to save more money for my future. I could never be persuaded that I had enough makeup or too much jewelry. I had so many shoes that my mom referred to me

16

as Imelda Marcos, who was famous for her enormous footwear collection. I was seldom questioned for owning too many clothes, as sisters and parents who had little regard for fashion rarely seemed to notice when I wore something new. And yes, I was a fashion major at Bluffton College. My enthusiasm for all things wearable was expected of me. My vintage pieces mixed with more classic J. Crew, combined with items from every store at every mall in the area gave me somewhat of a reputation. As did the vintage ball gown that I wore one Sunday to work in the fine jewelry department. A reputation for a costume-y wardrobe can be expensive to maintain!

Ada, Juliet, Medusa, and Ligeia; these are a few of the identities I assumed for myself during my three years living in Bluffton. I became the proud new owner of my first credit cards while I was a student. Major bank cards were still out of the question, as I had not yet built up a credit history. But my beloved and frequently shopped J.

17

Crew and Victoria's Secret were willing to take risks with me, as was the department store called Lazarus. Every week at college at least one new package arrived in my mailbox. I'll never forget the astonished expressions on my fellow students' faces when a full-sized sword and knight's helmet were delivered. A friend from Toledo, Ohio introduced me to their most upscale mall, where I raided the Chanel counter. Outings to the nearby Lima and Findlay malls were also a weekly occurrence, and necessary to prevent boredom.

The years in college were exciting times. I acquired a large circle of friends, and rid myself of the slacker boyfriend who couldn't keep up. I dreamed constantly of my career, and had no use for a boyfriend whose only solid plan for the future was to spend my money. *My money.* How little of it actually was. Some of what I used was store credit cards. Most of what I used was stolen from my parents' locked box or out of one of their many

18

other hiding places. Half of the thrill for me was listening for clues when I was at home and finding a new stash of cash. The other half was the knowledge, with racing pulse, that I was stealing money from the hardworking alcoholic dad who had told me he hated me. A very small percentage of what I spent was earned by my own efforts, working at the department store for minimum wage. Sad, but unfortunately true. How did it ever escalate to this level? It causes me twinges of pain to think back to these times, wishing that I could warn or help the younger version of myself.

Working in retail is an alluring trap for bored girls who have few real expenses of their own. The employee discount is tempting and is presented as such a good thing, but many stores require employees to open up a store credit card in order to receive their discount. My store was one of these, and so I was doomed from the beginning. I experienced the freedom of limitless spending, and my

19

poor mom had no clue how much trouble her oldest daughter was getting into while leading a more independent college life. I eagerly spent and charged all that I earned and more. This department store job, which I had for four years, delivered me willingly into the firm grip of shopping addiction. I needed my fix. I became fast friends with two older girls at work, bonded together by a common need for retail therapy. I was their eager pupil who has had a very sufficient head start.

It seems to be thought of as a cute vice, and it's expected in our United States culture for girls to be enthusiastic about shopping. Shopping is a commonly named hobby among females. But how wrong is this, since very few of us are truly wealthy enough to *spend* as a hobby? And so then we obviously *overspend*, and live beyond our means, as my friends and I most definitely did. My two shopping partners and I went to Dayton, Columbus, and Cincinnati together. They with their credit cards, and me with my amusing, stolen hundreds in cash. I was out of my league and didn't know it. I should have been learning to live on my own, on a tiny, modest budget, deprived of extravagant things, as my fellow students lived. Little did I know how detrimental this way of life would be to my future. How many times have I wished for the chance to go back into the past somehow and warn myself of the harm I was doing.

Chapter 3: At Long Last – Guilt!

Instead of living life as I was meant to, I played. My life

was a performance, I felt, and I certainly possessed enough

drama inside of myself to maintain this. I studied when I

needed to, created controversial projects for my fashion

and design classes, and shopped for further creative

fulfilment. Shopping filled empty, lonely time, and made

me feel as if I were already successful, like I was *someone*.

Tales of the outrageous lives and antics of current fashion

designers only fueled my neglect of reality. How many

false friendships did I form over the years, purely on the

basis of spending? I remember clearly staying in touch

with a girl I had met at work, a girl who had always gotten

under my skin in the most irritating way. I visited her quite

a few times after she went away for college, merely so she

would take me shopping. To my credit, I became very

generous with friends who had less, and gift-giving

became one of my favorite things to do, aside from

22

spending on myself. Extravagant Christmas and birthday presents, and little surprise gifts, just because. After all, I had plenty to spare, didn't I? And I think, perhaps, it helped to even out the guilt and the dark feelings that had begun to creep up on me. Was I actually starting to feel that it was wrong to steal from my parents? Why was it harder to be alone than ever? And why did I feel increasingly anxious when I shopped, and yet I couldn't resist the pull of the stores?

The most abominable feelings of all bombarded me in between shopping trips. When the pain of the present became too much to bear, I always felt a name change coming on. Occurring usually several times a year, a name change was inevitably accompanied by a purging of my wardrobe, and followed by a shopping binge to suit my slightly new identity. Vladimira, for instance, was very dark, and took me through a gothic phase. As Ada I liked to wear monogrammed jewelry and a black dress with a

23

lace collar. Juliet was inspired by the character in the movie "Heavenly Creatures", which a friend and I watched dozens of times, and adored because the characters in the movie were able to escape reality to another realm. My personality did not change enough for anyone else around me to really notice, other than for the phases of my wardrobe, and it was more of a creative compulsion, and not an actual separation of personalities. I always looked around me for new inspiration, and put a lot of deep thought into a new name choice, and what it would represent. How could I ever be content enough to just be Sarah – *the real me?*

I reached a point somewhere during my last two college years that I had begun to sneak around and hide my shopping habit much more guiltily than ever before. I understand now that my habit had developed into a full-fledged addiction, and I wonder if anything could have prevented it. At that point, a trip to a mall with a certain shopaholic friend always resulted in no fewer than three pairs of new shoes. My own secret visits to the outlet malls or to a more upscale location of my home department store (where they actually had some *designer* clothes) were becoming more frequent. It seemed like I never had enough money, and each time now that I took cash from my parents was always supposed to be the last. I remember on one occasion carrying a wad of $800, still smelling of hair salon (my dad's business), into my workplace to make a payment on my credit card. After all, I consoled myself, when I get my fabulous high-paying fashion job after graduation, I will no longer need my credit cards. What a long and treacherous road I had ahead of me, and how jaded I was!

During my senior year at college, a bit of my fantasy world came crashing down around me. My mom confronted me about the large amounts of money that disappeared very obviously whenever I was home for the weekend. I lied repeatedly when she accused me, but inwardly I planned an escape. One final time to take as much money as I could, and then flee the state or the country, and build a new life. The soul-less part of me never considered how this selfish move would hurt my family. My mom's accusations were the absolute worst case scenario, and it was the major, inevitable event that I had dreaded for so many years. I was certain that she would disown me, and the large amounts of money that I wasn't capable of living without instantly became a thing of the past. I had gotten away with stealing and spending larger and larger amounts until it was obvious that I would be caught. I had become almost intentionally reckless, and it was definitely a cry for help.

In her mind, my mom could not conceive that one of her daughters would willingly engage in such dishonest and criminal behavior. She had assumed for so many years that my dad, in his alcoholic state, was doing something

26

else with the money. I knew this, counted on it, and was comfortable with the idea that my dad would take the blame. When it came to a point that my mom finally had no other choice but to face the reality that I was responsible for so much missing money, she should have called the police. I expected her to. Astonishingly, she kept the secret between the two of us. She listened to my reasons and excuses and pleas. And then she forgave me.

I wish I could claim that after this point I never again stole from anyone but myself. I was grateful, yet terrified of the fresh start my mom gave me. She generously presented me with undeserved birthday presents a few weeks later, and understood, I think, my need to punish my dad. She was never the one that I intended to hurt, and it saddened me to no end that I had caused her such tremendous grief. How could I live with the pain of this guilt? At this age I never stopped to think about receiving forgiveness from

God. Or forgiving myself, for that matter. Perhaps if I had, I would not have had so much additional pain to bury.

I used my last year of college to attempt to learn to live on a budget. I sincerely did try. But the unfortunate fact was that my store credit cards already had their hooks sunk into me too firmly to be easily removed, and I had not expected to be faced with such an intense challenge. I had relied on my stolen cash to make monthly payments on my credit cards, but my weekend job just wasn't enough on its own. I took a small amount of money from my parents' locked box just two more times, as it only took a matter of minutes for me to figure out the most recent combination. I also delighted in the fact that my drunken father thought he was so clever about where he hid the box, and even after I stopped stealing money, I was always up for the challenge of finding it again. Guilt overwhelmed me. My mom's compassion and attempt to understand my motives made me want to come clean. She did another amazing

28

thing, and paid off my store credit cards. A doubly fresh start that I most assuredly did not deserve!

Somehow or another I made it through my senior year of college without creating any more debt. I did, however, spend every dime that I earned at my part-time job in the most frivolous manner. There were still frequent trips to the local malls. The types of clothing I was bought at this time left much to be desired in the way of quality, but was reasonably inexpensive or "disposable" clothing, as I refer to it these days. I went for quantity and shock value, and this was easy to achieve on a budget. Black plastic dresses, faux fur skirts, rubber snakes worn in my hair (as Medusa, of course), tights of all colors and patterns, and a white faux fur coat that I spray painted neon green. In the sheltered Mennonite college town of Bluffton, it was easier to cut back on spending and just make my wardrobe a little more outrageous. I remember drawing a crowd at the Dollar Store one afternoon, spending fifty dollars' worth of quarters in a gumball machine, emptying it out, just to get the ring I wanted. I never thought to compare the quality of the plastic ring with a ring that I might actually pay $50 for. Still, I knew there was much more shopping out there in the world. I only had to hold off until graduation and my first real job to begin spending my paychecks.

Unfortunately for Juliet, as I was known during the spring of 1998, life and the prosperous new career did not work out as smoothly as I had expected it to. During the summer after graduation I continued to work at the local department store, spinning tales of an imaginary move to Madagascar, visiting my friends in Bluffton and Columbus quite often, and job searching the best that I knew how. The type of job I was looking for, I didn't really know how to go about finding. It was a huge reality check that as a college graduate with a fashion degree, the design firms and fashion houses were not actually in pursuit of *me*. I

30

did know that I was sick to death of working in retail and customer service. I had finished college with a Bachelor of Arts in Apparel and Textile Merchandising and Design. But my small private college had failed to equip me very well for either design or merchandising. I became one of a large group of fashion degree graduates who ended up, out of desperation, floating right back into clothing retail, where we had started before college. I certainly didn't need a college degree for the minimum wage job that I finally landed at a Columbus, Ohio United Colors of Benetton boutique. A friend from my classes at Bluffton College had been hired as the assistant manager, so I had hope for moving up in the ranks. In the meantime, I settled into my new apartment and my job as Isabella, entertaining my restless soul by studying languages, and by exploring the endless shopping possibilities of my new city.

31

My college wardrobe, of course, was completely unsuitable for my new lifestyle. My life as a full-time retail sales girl was all about updating my wardrobe, one paycheck at a time. Soon enough I began using my lunch breaks to explore all of the other stores at the mall. One way or another, I acquired each piece I desired at my home store. And then, by trading associate discounts with employees of other stores like Banana Republic and Victoria's Secret, I became even more immersed in the shopping culture of mall employees. It wasn't long before an emergency pair of grey knee-high faux snakeskin boots became the first purchase on a new Macy's charge card. Many additional purchases followed in the months ahead. Sadly enough, I often ended up at the mall on my days off, scouting out future purchases, and memorizing the inventory of all of my favorite stores.

I became well-acquainted with Columbus' downtown City Center Mall, which I adored for its Guess store, Marshall

Field's, a small Louis Vuitton boutique, and a second
United Colors of Benetton store. My former college
roommate and I were weekly, and sometimes daily
customers of the strip mall that was within walking
distance of her apartment. There was a reliable Banana
Republic and a Victoria's Secret, where something new
was always in stock. It became evident that my friendship
with this friend had a solid foundation of spending. We
both loved exotic food, and at least weekly new items of
clothing were a must. Eating out with my friend so often
was a huge strain on my "budget", and I remember
appealing to her for time together that didn't involve
spending. My friend earned more and more with her new
promotion at work, and I continued to live paycheck to
paycheck with my unfulfilling minimum wage job.

Chapter 4: A Superficial Lifestyle

Try as I might, I could not manage to curb my spending. I began to see less of my high-rolling friend, as she gradually exchanged me for a group of people with well-paying jobs. Our incomes, it seemed, made us incompatible. Each week, I found myself at the local laundromat, alone, which also meant that I would make my customary weekly visit to TJ Maxx, just a short walk away. Effortlessly forgetting about my laundry, I was often lost for hours in TJ Maxx, combing the store for a treasured item. I could not face the disappointment of leaving the store empty-handed. I often found things to put on layaway, and clearly remember emptying out my checking account on more than one occasion for an item that might have been too big or too small, but was "perfect", and I had to have it. In fact, I could not imagine living my life without it. And then, starving, exhausted, usually with a pounding headache, I would reluctantly head back to collect the wrinkled laundry that I hoped was still waiting for me.

At this time in my life, I believe my name had changed to Heizhenzou, which means "black pearl" in Chinese. I happily acquired a new boyfriend who was as materialistic as I was. We shopped every weekend, buying gifts for ourselves as well as for each other. I with my credit cards, and he with money from his dad. To my boyfriend and I, and the girls I worked with, appearance was everything. New purchases made by friends and coworkers inspired both jealousy and competition, and motivated me to make purchases of my own. It was an obviously never-ending cycle, but in my eyes I just needed to earn more money. My apartment remained embarrassingly unfurnished, but my wardrobe had grown with leaps and bounds.

It was the greed for more clothing that helped me to get a full-time job at the shoe store Enzo Angiolini. I continued to work part-time at Benetton in order to keep my discount, but my college friend had abandoned the store for another job a few months ago, giving up on ever being promoted. Now, not only did I have to keep up with buying all of the things I had on hold at Benetton, but it seemed that every day a new pair of shoes caught my attention. Green boots, black heels, and sandals the shade of the teal blue Louis Vuitton bag that I couldn't afford. My head swam with all of my options, and if I couldn't afford my "fix' at the mall, I'd head to one of many thrift stores on a rare day off.

I was working hard, underpaid, and dreaded going to work each day. I realized during this first year after college that the only thing I liked about retail work was constantly being surrounded by material things. Following is an excerpt from my journal during this time. "Always on my mind is what I am going to eat or buy next. I have to find a way out of this life! I just need an escape. I need to live

36

a different life that I dwell on, constantly. My brain never seems to come alive anymore. *When* am I creatively challenged? *Something* must happen! I am feeling so desperate again". Clearly, my creativity was being satisfied, but not fulfilled, by shopping. I couldn't manage to slow it down long enough to realize what the problem was. How many people today, I wonder, are facing the same issue?

I loved the ever-changing merchandise at my retail jobs, but was too introverted to ever be very good at or comfortable with customer service. By the end of a work-day in customer service, my nerves were frazzled, and I was an anti-social grouch. I craved freedom and quiet and lots of alone time. Day after day of the type of work that demanded an outgoing personality took a serious toll on my mental health, making me extremely anxious and moody. Feeling somewhat lost, I began job searching for entry-level office work outside of the mall. I couldn't imagine how delightful it would be not to have to work weekends and holidays. How soothing it would be not to have to talk to strangers all day long. Also, I realized more than ever now, both guiltily and helplessly, that my entire life revolved around shopping. My dream job was out there waiting to be found, and I didn't want to lose my focus, surrounded by so many stylish, expensive distractions.

Just before the holidays in 1999, I landed the first of what would turn out to be a series of office jobs. I grew bored with the work within months of acquiring each new job, as answering the phone and filing and making labels did not fulfill any of my creative needs. I continued to turn to shopping after dull days of work. Sitting all day at a desk drained and frustrated me, and I found any number of reasons to leave my seat just to walk around for a few minutes. Then, of course, I wasn't at my desk when the phone rang, which understandably aggravated bosses and

38

coworkers. Also, I quickly found out that there was little respect in secretarial work. Clients and coworkers treated me like I didn't matter, and seemed like they assumed I was brainless and married to someone who paid my bills. This was my interpretation. More than likely, it was my own low self-esteem over my lack of career that produced these feelings of inadequacy. And the more frustrated I became from work, the more I looked for excitement and relief from shopping.

Lonely Sunday afternoons were so depressing after my boyfriend left to drive back to school for the week. I had moved into a tiny apartment, so it's not like there was yardwork or cleaning to do, and in this particular place I had no space to work on creative projects. Those dreaded Sundays – how I hated them– and they led to more shopping mishaps than I could possibly count. I wrote in my journal, "If I let the depression take me, it will be all over. I will run away somewhere and live inside of my

39

imagination. Insanity promises to give me a better life if reality does not. My mind has so many ideas and worlds inside. I might get sucked in if I am unable to convert it into reality". I dreaded the thought of someone reading my self-centered journal if I died, going so far as to hide it in the trunk of my car if I had friends over. The truth about me, what a selfish and horrible person I was, was a secret that I was determined to keep to myself. I yearned to get back to my healthier interests like photography, fossils, plants, history, and writing. Monday morning was always too close for comfort, and I wondered longingly if I would ever find my place in the career world, or at least something for the time being that didn't drive me stark raving mad!

Somewhere during the time of my transition from retail to office work, my dear mom responded to the despair of my debt and again paid off all of my credit cards. So often, at the end of another tragic Sunday, I would call her in tears.

40

Alone or with friends, I would inevitably end up in a clothing store, and I would inevitably find things that I could not possibly live without. When I claim that I could not live without these new items, I truly and sincerely mean it. Without shopping, it felt as if I would give up completely. Shopping was to motivation to go to work in the morning, and it was the hours of my life that I gave to a job I couldn't stand that would bring something new into my life so that I could make it through the next work week. I was physically and emotionally dependent on bringing new items into my life. It was almost as if another part of me took over my body and mind during the shopping. The thrill of the hunt would make my pulse race. I looked forward to nothing like I looked forward to spending. I look back at these years and realize that my boyfriend could only get so close to me before shopping interfered. During his weekend visits, he had begun to like to stay in rather than to go out shopping. I was extremely

41

restless trying to stay at home in my small apartment, and would grow more and more agitated until he would leave, at which time I would go out and shop.

So much built-up need and stifled pain would cause me to fight against my sensible side, and I would quickly and savagely shred the receipts and price tags once I got home, to prevent the more reality-based part of me from returning the items. Then hours later I would succumb to regret. It was never so strong as a split personality, but rather like my good and evil sides battling over saving me or destroying me. I think that many people with an addiction can identify with this.

I did end up returning merchandise, and often, because I had previously destroyed them, without a receipt or price tag, and along with some kind of elaborate, fabricated story to tell the sales associate. It was a challenge, and perhaps a bit of revenge against the retail jobs in which I had also had to play the dreaded role of sales associate. Last week or last month's item many times become a store credit towards my next purchase. In between paychecks and desperate for something new, I often schemed and plotted, negotiating my current wardrobe and sacrificing one thing for something "better". I was just one of an entire group of shopaholic girls who bought, exchanged, and returned merchandise as if it were a part-time job. I never owned my own ticket gun in order to switch price tags, but I was aware of many girls who did. Most stores will give a price adjustment within a week to a month after a purchase, if an item would happen to go on sale. It was just as likely for me to get a price adjustment after thirty days as it was to tire of an item and return it, worn only one time. It was incredibly disappointing to wear something for the second time, and would set a depressing tone for the entire day. It gave me a sense of being poor and defeated, and I much preferred the successful feeling of wearing something new.

An excerpt from my journal around this time reads, "Svetlana and I went to the outlet malls yesterday. I am horrified by the way I spend money! I really have *no* control over my habit, and I always think that *if I buy this one last thing*, then I am caught up, and there is nothing else that I want. But I always go somewhere and see something else that would make me happier. I always worry that my clothes/shoes are getting worn out, and that I will not be able to buy it when I need it." Another entry reads, "All of my focus in life right now is staying thin and what to buy next. I am trapped in a cycle and I really cannot stop. And I haven't got any more money saved than before, plus I have more credit card debt. I stay awake at night with my pulse racing, dwelling on what to buy next or how to keep myself from eating so much. It is all so complicated and disgusting! Even when I am with

44

Alan, I find myself blocking all sensation of him out, and focusing on shopping or the lunch that we haven't eaten yet. It is so sad, and he has been so devoted to me lately".

By the year 2001, I had had absolutely enough of my stale office job, sitting all day, answering the phone, and doing light accounting. My nerves were shattered, and the unused creativity welled up inside of me and caused major self-destruction. I knew that I was destined to work in a creative field, and held onto an intense dream that I would one day have my own business. I constantly assigned myself creative projects, such as hand sewing an entire jacket from upholstery fabric, or designing a shoe and building a prototype. I had been doing such dull work since college that I was afraid my creativity would vanish, and it almost hurt to call it back. I certainly wasn't on the right path working as an administrative assistant, and looked very forward to the jewelry making and copper enameling classes I enrolled in during evenings. The next

45

logical step seemed to be to go back to school. While I really would have loved to study jewelry design for four years, or to get a Master's Degree in color theory, I had to consider practicality and cost. After doing thorough research I concluded that either photography or graphic design would be compatible with my fashion degree and, based on the job market at the time, it would be easy enough to find work in either field.

Chapter 5: Back to School

I knew that I was serious enough about accomplishing my goal of going back to school, but it was vital to get away from the distraction of shopping in Columbus. I ended up moving to Dayton, Ohio, enrolling in Sinclair College, and sharing an apartment with my boyfriend, who had just finished his Bachelor's Degree. Before I left Columbus, I used my vacation pay to buy a few "classic" clothing items, as well as to pay off the small credit card balance I had allowed to accumulate since my mom had paid off my other cards.

Determined, and with great focus, I buried myself in my graphic design school work and found a part-time job at a nearby health food store. I had taken out loans for school, and allowed myself an occasional clothing purchase online or at one of the local malls. I seldom went out shopping, which seemed to help control my cravings, and attempted as much as possible to gain fulfillment from the creative work that kept me so busy. Each time I received a deposit from my student loan, I made a trip to Columbus to shop. There was a drastic difference in the people in Dayton as compared to Columbus inhabitants. Fewer people in Dayton seemed to care much about shopping, and although I was still very much concerned with appearance and how I dressed, I was surrounded by girls in outdated jeans, sweatpants, baseball caps, and with no makeup. I was astonished to find that I could wear the same outfits over and over again without feeling too insecure. Could it really be that there were more important things in life? Of course I knew that there were and what these things were supposed to be. Money doesn't buy happiness, and the best things in life are free, etc. Sadly, I just didn't understand it.

Living in Dayton that first year with my boyfriend, I was very happy. I found that I really missed my friends and my social life, and didn't realize just how deprived of

48

shopping and eating out that I had become. Dayton didn't have many of the delicious ethnic restaurants that my friends and I had often frequented in Columbus, and so I made it my mission to learn to cook these foods for myself. I would like to look back and conclude that I wasn't overspending, but because of my part-time job, I soon became obsessed with the health food scene and the unattainable perfection it offered. Rarely a day went by when I didn't make a purchase at work. New spices, meat alternatives, vitamins and supplements, along with more environmentally friendly but more expensive beauty products all competed for my attention. It didn't seem as serious as shopping for clothing, but my addiction was still alive.

It felt really gratifying to be so focused on my goal, but somewhere in the back of my mind I was trying to stop noticing how outdated and how worn out my wardrobe was becoming, or how outdated and how worn out I

49

thought it had become. It took all of my willpower to delay my shopping cravings until I found the well-paying job I knew I would get once I finished school again. At this point in time I was at least not using credit cards. My life progressed remarkably smoothly for the first three quarters of school. So, as a reward, and with a tax refund check sitting in my bank account, I agreed with some well-justified hesitation to join a friend for a trip to New York City.

My visit to NYC was a major turning point I like to refer to as sensory overload!

There I was in one of the most shopping-oriented places in the entire world. Though we did engage in many touristy activities, such as visiting the United Nations, I remember trembling with anticipation as we quickly entered and exited many fascinating stores that I longed to have time to actually shop in and try things on. Two fantastic trips to

Chinatown for "designer" handbags had not quenched my thirst, but, much to my incredible dismay, the friends I had travelled with did not share my love of shopping to quite the same extent. When I left New York City and headed back to Dayton to my busy and disciplined life, I felt unsatisfied. The small flame for shopping that I had managed to keep tame for the past year now exploded into roaring flames.

With one year of classes left before I was fully prepared to accept one of the well-paid graphic design jobs that I was positive I would find, I allowed myself to open up a new credit card. Almost ravenously, I planned a trip to some nearby outlet malls. Shopping certainly, was the one thing I looked forward to most about finishing my schooling. It was at the halfway point in my Associate's Degree program that I admitted to myself that I did not enjoy graphic design. I loved and thrived at any type of 3-D design that I was required to do, but it was sadly

51

frustrating to note that I did not have a knack for computers and printers, or a very good eye for the typical commercial graphic design. I grew bored and anxious with all of the hours of sitting and staring at the computer, as my second year of classes required just that. No longer did I have all of the immense new creative stimulation of my first year of classes. I was busy, but bored, and I poured all of my un-stimulated creativity back into shopping.

Just as I had been in Columbus, I grew restless with weekends that did not involve shopping. My boyfriend, now working full-time and in graduate school, became very cranky and stingy, and buried himself in his martial arts during his free time. I remember feeling incredibly isolated living in Dayton. My boyfriend's new social group was much more conservative than the large group of friends I had met in college and while living in Columbus. I still grasped onto the big dream of having my own

52

business, but the people around me seemed not to have any dreams at all outside of the standard marriage and children. Looking back, and having been through way more life experiences, I wonder now how many of those people had tried to attain significant dreams and had failed. I know now how common it is to fail, and why it is such a remarkable thing when a business or another lifelong dream does actually succeed!

My career, I believed, would buy me independence from a man. This tended to be an important goal for me to pay my own way in life, and likely because my dad had assured me that it would not be possible. I supposed that I would work at an average-salaried graphic design job until I had worked up the courage, knowledge, and savings to launch what was to be my real career – my fulfilling career. My boyfriend seemed to be absorbing all of the conservative ideals of his coworkers and friends in his martial arts classes and at his workplace. I felt us drifting

53

apart as I kept my eye on my big goal, which he seemed to understand less and less. He mocked my design projects and didn't quite get the fact that an average life and an average job, as well as taking second place to him in life, were never going to make me happy. He did not appreciate my creativity for what it was, and began to expect me to blend in with his new set of friends. I would never be able to be myself with them...especially if they found out about my name changes. I figured that it was best to keep the real me to myself, and so I craved solitude, and I often persuaded my boyfriend to go out with his friends without me, as I preferred to shop or work on a project on my own. Now, not only did my creativity isolate me from our social group in Dayton, but my shopping adventures provided me with an escape from the boyfriend for whom I could never be perfect or normal enough.

Although I could tell that my shopping was a growing concern for my boyfriend, he became increasingly obsessed with my appearance, my weight, and the fact that I was not tan. I remember explaining to him that I planned to be frugal and purchase drugstore makeup while I was in school, and he told me that I could go and then find a cheap boyfriend as well. Ever-sensitive to his criticisms of a scuff on my shoes or another jab at my "outdated" wardrobe, I became hyper-aware of anything that might look worn out. Bras, panties, socks, shoes --- I felt that the only way I had left to please my boyfriend was through my appearance. It was almost as if flaws in my wardrobe betrayed flaws within me. I panicked at the possibility of an item of clothing wearing out, with no back-up replacement piece. I had to have lots of extra black pants, a large supply of black skirts and shirts, heeled sandals in every color, and an endless collection of black and brown shoes and boots in a variety of heel heights and toe shapes.

55

I simply did not know where to stop with the extras and replacements. The fear of not having enough to wear, or of not being able to find something to match what I did have, grew monumental. A pair of panties or tights snagging would send me into a panic – pulse racing – until I could replace the damaged items as well as purchase back-ups. My boyfriend's snide remarks about a small mark on a nearly new pair of brown boots devastated me. He actually asked me if they were old! This sent me into a frantic shopping spree. Anywhere in Dayton that sold boots – DSW, Parisian, TJ Maxx, etc. I dedicated hours to shopping online whenever I was alone. Shameful box after box of boots arrived at our apartment after that comment. I'm not even sure my boyfriend noticed. The only compliments I received from him were regarding my appearance, strangely echoing the only compliments I remember ever receiving from my dad. I sought my boyfriend's approval wholeheartedly, and always tried to

56

be the best dressed and accessorized girl in the room, wherever we went together. It wasn't uncommon for him to tell me how I had rated when we left a gathering of people, and some part of me needed the challenge of winning the approval that was becoming more and more impossible to get. I knew to keep silent, when we were among his friends. After all, I didn't want to embarrass him by voicing my unusual opinions. The only self-esteem I must have had at that point in time came as a direct result of my appearance. It is no wonder that I was forever on an endless search for items that promised to make me look better than I currently did.

Chapter 6: Emptiness to Fill

I somehow managed to make it to the end of the two-year visual communications program at Sinclair College. Full of relief and a strong sense of destiny, I *knew* that I would quickly find a well-paying graphic design job. I believed in my success with such intensity, and wanted to demonstrate my faith, so I quit my job at the health food store. I had continued my bad habit of buying one of anything and everything. I began job searching (and shopping) full-time, believing that God would reward my courageous act of faith. With hopes for a new job on the horizon, my boyfriend and I signed a year lease for a townhouse. I hadn't been sure at all that our relationship was in good enough shape for us to continue living together. I had proposed that we should separate for a while in order to re-evaluate the direction we each wanted to take next. But my boyfriend assured me that he wanted to spend the rest of his life with me. I was not sure that this was what *I* wanted, since his constant criticisms of me made for unpleasant company. I explained to him that he needed to learn to treat me with more respect and kindness, if we were to stay together. I knew I was no longer in love with him, but I did love him tremendously as a friend and as family. To hurt him in any way was something I felt incapable of. I felt that it was a noble and giving gesture on my part to agree to a secret marriage, so that he could start the process of applying for his green card. Actually, the thought of marriage made me want to run away. I told my new husband that he had three years to improve his behavior towards me. If our situation hadn't improved by then, I would divorce him. If he had changed for the better at the end of the three years, we could have a small wedding and let our family members know about it.

With a new place to live came all types of new demands for shopping. I purchased a sofa, chair, and a coffee table on credit…excited to live a more sophisticated adult life, and somehow certain that these new things made it all more real. Our three-floor townhouse looked rather empty with only the furnishings brought over from our two-bedroom apartment, and so when my mom sent me a surprise check in the mail as a reward for finishing school, I immediately used it to order another piece of furniture. It would have been smart to save the money or to pay off some of my debt. Especially since I hadn't yet found a job.

My days were full of cooking, job searching, cleaning, and, of course, making my rounds to all of my local shopping haunts. I was relieved to break this routine when I accepted a design assistant position at a local advertising agency in late 2003. While I started out at the front desk, and helped the designers with small projects, it was with the understanding that I would be promoted to a design position within the year. Boredom quickly plagued me,

60

without much assigned work to do. It was a shock to my system to lose my free time, being required to sit again for eight hours a day. Chained to the phone and isolated in the front office away from my coworkers, the internet was my only friend. I passed the time by shopping online, writing a short story, and working on my portfolio. I was grateful for the job, but the hours of each day crawled by alarmingly slowly. Sadly, I only looked forward to shopping.

One month after settling into my new job, my personal life came crashing down around me. I returned home from work on Halloween evening and immediately sensed something intense as I touched the door handle to go inside. My husband of two months was waiting, drink in hand, to explain that he needed time alone, and that he wanted to break up with me. It wasn't me, it was him. This revelation came only a week after his confession that a flirtatious coworker had kissed him in the basement of

61

their office building. He had vomited from guilt, and had pledged his love for me. He had claimed again to want to be with me forever. I don't think I was particularly touched or elated when he professed his love for me, but I do remember the extreme shock that his words caused me on the day of our breakup in 2003. Where was I going to live, and would my small salary be sufficient to pay all of my bills? My new job had kept us apart even more than when I had been in school, allowing much more distance to settle in between us. My husband was always grouchy, and was working all of the late nights and weekends at the office that are stereotypical of an affair. Still, I believed what he told me, that he needed a one-year break. I thought back to a crumbled pro and con list I had found in his trash can some time ago. The subject was *me*. The pros were only two; beautiful and good sense of style. The list of things against me was so much longer. They were all things that I had no control over, like allergies, asthma,

62

and being introverted. It was a window into the cruel and superficial way that he judged me, and I wish I had seen it as a sign of things to come.

I had not one shred of confidence left inside of me when I moved out of our home two weeks later. He wanted me nearby for safety reasons, and begged me not to date anyone he didn't approve of. I focused on a fresh start, so sure that we would be back together at the end of a year, and threw myself into furnishing my second new apartment that fall. Another intense workout for my credit cards. I was crushed inside, and felt so betrayed and caught off guard. I was determined to adopt a positive attitude about the situation, and was grateful for a job that had the potential to take me places. But pretending to be positive was only half of my battle. There was a huge aching hole inside of me, and my shopping addiction spun more out of control than perhaps it had ever been. I believed that I was drawing comfort from God, since I had

63

joined a weekly Bible study and prayed faithfully. I read my Bible every day, but the only thing that truly calmed me was shopping.

My ex spent a lot of time at my new apartment, and planned with me our move back in together in one year. I believed what he told me, and kept my head above water with a constant flood of packages delivered to my workplace. A large part of me must have been in denial about the huge debt I was growing. As long as I was happy, stayed positive, and could make my minimum payments, things would work out, I convinced myself. As a grand gesture, I allowed my ex to choose my newest name....Leila. But it never fit, and I never felt like her. His grand gesture in reciprocation was a large part of that December spent with him, his parents, and his sister, who were visiting from Croatia. I felt honored to meet them, and took his mom and sister on several shopping trips, as this was my specialty, after all. His sister assured me that

64

her brother loved me and that we would end up together. I couldn't have agreed with her more.

I cringe to look back at the excesses of my life during this time. Paris Hilton's "Simple Life" reality show was on TV, and for some reason the publicity of her own shopping excesses fueled my addiction and gave it credibility. My wardrobe was crowded with Forever 21 junk and low quality pieces from Macy's junior's department. I could not rest until I had jeweled and strappy sandals in every shade of every color. I spent hours of my days at work examining designer handbags and studying their fake counterparts. I then paid hundreds of dollars apiece for AAA quality imitations shipped straight from China. Every new item I acquired fed my appetite and created a craving and a need for more new items. Dishes, pillows, sheet sets----I was trying to bury the pain that I would have been so much better off just living through....if only I had known how. Oddly enough, the more I shopped and spent, the more I ate that winter. I consumed thousands upon thousands of calories in an attempt to satisfy a hunger that ultimately was probably caused by loneliness and guilt.

Spring arrived that year, along with quite a few new pieces of furniture that I had ordered online. I was determined to buy myself the happiness and contentment that my ex was never able to give me. That same spring, not only did I learn that my dad was dying from lung cancer, but I was also unexpectedly laid off from my job. My ex began to grow more distant and reluctantly admitted to me that he was now somewhat more involved with the coworker who had kissed him. Absolutely sick with despair, I began staying several nights a week at my parents' house. I volunteered my services two days a week at the advertising agency, determined to keep a bit of normalcy in my life, and wanting to be available for rehire when the opportunity came. My ex assured me that it was only a matter of time before he broke up with his mistress. He

66

was clearly not in love with her, and seemed puzzled about how to end things with her. He persuaded me to remain married to him since we would likely end up together again soon.

Weeks of unemployment in 2004 became months. While I dreaded the loneliness of living in my apartment in Dayton a few days each week, I looked forward to the shopping fix that I would inevitably reward myself with. In between job searching and interviews, one day out of the blue I received a phone call from a female who identified herself as my ex's girlfriend. My body numbed with horror as she revealed to me the many ways that she and he had deceived me. She almost seemed amused, enjoying my pain and insisting that we meet in person. She was equally caught off guard to learn that my ex had been leading a double life with me, and had no idea that I had spent the holidays with him and his family. She wasn't aware that we still saw each other. It saddened me to think that it was

67

I had who had chosen his shirt and tie on the afternoon that I had encouraged him to meet her for coffee, believing at the time that it was an innocent meeting of coworkers. He had been completely open in the beginning, showing me her emails to him, and laughing at the thought that she may have liked him.

Though I had given my best efforts, I had not managed to become perfect enough to keep our relationship intact. He had loved me, once, but familiarity apparently bred contempt in our case, and I had been too close to him for too long. The stunning effect of this betrayal caused anguish in me like nothing else I had ever felt. How was it possible to live through this amount of pain? This intense situation, combined with my job loss, and then my dad's death a few weeks later, made me unrecognizable to myself. That summer I became Sakhmet. I was an Egyptian slave who languished in despair under the relentless Egyptian sun. Crawling miserably on scorched

68

knees in an attempt to escape my circumstances, my frequent tears were the only relief from the shriveled, dehydrated life I now led.

Shopping, my loyal heroine, came swiftly to my rescue. The first purchase as Sakhmet was a 14K gold pendant of the Egyptian cat goddess of the same name. A name change did not feel legitimate until I had bought a piece of jewelry to represent that period of my life. Though it would be more than two years before I recovered from my intense losses, I am ashamed to admit that purchases are what got me through the long and isolated days. I received unemployment checks for six months, and my mom gave me monthly checks to cover my rent and credit card bills. Those frightening credit cards, whose minimum payments terrorized me each month, became my best and most reliable friends.

I stopped volunteering at my old job, since any hopes of being rehired evaporated when the company disintegrated later that year. I made weekly nerve-wracking visits to my Dayton apartment to gradually pack my belongings, and always with the ulterior motive of visiting one of the malls. Much of what I purchased during this time would remain unworn in my closet, and therefore never earned its keep.

By the fall of 2004, I had all of my belongings moved into storage, and lived full-time in Piqua. Each day I would watch my dedicated mom go to work, grieving for her lost husband, while I, in a dark cloud of depression, remained at home for a steady routine of job searching, cleaning, cooking, and shopping online. Just as the intensity of my shopping continued, so did the enormity of my appetite. I had so much pain to numb with both dollars and calories. I have never eaten so much in my life as I did during this time, and I believe that there is a direct relation to these being my peak spending years. My size two body expanded to a six, and I used this excuse for more and more secret shopping trips to Dayton and Columbus, to replace the clothes that no longer fit me. I was not happy to have gained weight, but couldn't rid myself of the clothes I had worn during my life in Dayton fast enough. It was my way of discarding the part of me who was experiencing so much pain.

Merchandise from my shopping trips remained in the trunk of my car until I could slip the bags into the house without my mom or sister noticing. I would occasionally be bold enough to have a package delivered to our home address, but it would inevitably, and much to my guilty dismay, be discovered first by my mom or my sister. Piles of packages from J. Crew, Zappos, Sephora, Victoria's Secret, and Sanrio regularly arrived at a friend's house, awaiting my weekly visit. This friend, too, was a shopping addict, and together we binged on Urban

71

Outfitters, MAC cosmetics, and high-priced international fashion magazines. Hello Kitty was a childish craving that we both indulged in, and even a trip to a Chinese grocery store or thrift store resulted in major overspending.

Aside from my time-consuming shopping, I job-searched in earnest each day, wanting desperately for my life to move on and to have a fresh start. Each seemingly useless resume I submitted and every discouraging job interview I went on injected me with a powerful dose of rejection. These combined with the knowledge that my ex was establishing some kind of a relationship with his mistress (seamlessly from our relationship) produced a pain so intense that I was unable to handle it. The only protection I had from the depression and anxiety was hours of online shopping and multiple weekly purchases. Each item I bought was intended to be the last. Just one more, and then I'll stop, I reassured myself. But each final purchase was disappointing in the fact that it was only a temporary

72

barrier from the pain. Because I was attempting to shield myself from pain that God had likely intended me to live through with his comfort and guidance (pain is, in fact, quite natural and necessary in life), I became more and more hyper-sensitive to everything and everyone around me. An expression on someone's face, a slightly harsh or impatient tone of voice, or words that my paranoid mind twisted out of context, easily sent me into a downward spiral. When I was upset, it was unbearable to think that I wasn't able to buy something to soothe myself. The thought that I was unemployed and had zero income was a reality I couldn't face. I absolutely panicked to even consider or imagine not shopping or not being *able* to shop. My credit cards kept up the façade ---- they were a lie that I told myself daily, and in doing this, I robbed myself in the future.

It was never long after purchasing the final thing that I had to have, that I felt the indescribable restlessness inside of me resurfacing. It was literally as if a shopping demon had possessed me, physically and mentally. I became unbearable to be around, incredibly moody, distracted, and agitated. I could not sleep. If I allowed myself to imagine making a purchase, a calming euphoria washed through me. It was not uncommon for me to sneak downstairs to the computer at night to spend hours filtering through the hundreds of shoes in my size on Zappos.com. It was as if I had an undying curiosity to discover what my next new purchase would be. And of course, once my innocent browsing of online stores produced the next must-have item, it was only a matter of time before my mind had built it up into such a life or death situation that I had no choice but to purchase it.

One year into my unemployment, I was hired part-time at a department store. I had not even made it through all of the paid training before I realized with great horror that I had already compiled an enormous list of must-have items

74

from around the store. I was really out of control! My paycheck was already spent before I had even earned it, and I planned to bring my credit card to work in order to reward myself for taking another job that was the opposite of what would make me happy. I had multiple panic attacks as a result of this realization, and was confused as to what would be the right thing to do. I understood that this job would serve to increase my debt and would continue to feed my shopping problem. Since this was the only work I had been able to find after a year of searching and interviewing, I was faced with the severity of my addiction. It truly was no different than an unemployed alcoholic finding much-needed work in a bar. I had hoped that there would be no temptations for me at the department store. It was not a store I ever shopped at, but it was troubling how appealing their so-so quality merchandise appeared when I was looking for a fix. A fix to calm the huge anxiety I felt about "being on stage" at

75

the busy cash register, forced to talk to strangers when I just wanted to be alone. A fix to drown out the humiliation and pain of a minimum wage part-time job in clothing retail – right where I was before I had ever gone to school. It seemed that I had made it nowhere in life, even with six years of partially unpaid for college under my belt.

Desperate for help for all of my many problems and masses of un-dealt with pain, I sought counseling. I remember the overwhelmed expression on my counselor's face as she listened during the first few sessions. It seemed to me that I was mentally ill, not being able to stop shopping, with my tremendous depression and anxiety over the nothingness of my life growing in proportion every day. I felt so passionately and dramatically about all of the great loss I had experienced in such a short amount of time. I had lost the ability to function well or to identify realistically with the outside world, as I had become extremely fragile.

76

My counselor concluded that I suffered from post-traumatic stress syndrome. I could not cope with my life, so I shopped and I ate. I had a colossal amount of frustration built up over the lack of a career. The fulfillment that I believed I would have experienced from a creative job was now channeled into my wardrobe as well as into cooking gourmet meals. Weekly sessions with my counselor, who really was quite baffled as to how to help me, and admitted so, made me realize that boredom, pain, and stress gave me an inexplicable need for something, which could just as easily have been drugs or alcohol. Relief, in the form of something new, which, in turn, enabled me to dispose of something older and therefore saturated with pain. I had learned to dispose of everything in my life in search of the next better thing – people, jobs, clothes, furniture, jewelry, music, and makeup. A new pair of shoes was an effortless and fun way to create a bit of a new identity in my life, leaving behind a trail of older,

77

(outdated?), and freshly rejected items. It was an expensive habit. The unhappier I became with my failure and with the circumstances my life had brought me into, obviously the more shopping I needed to do in order to feel sane. Like any addict, I became desensitized to a new purchase or fix, and the problem got worse as I spent more money, had less credit available to use, and was dangerously close to not being able to make my minimum monthly payments.

Months went by. I talked, my counselor listened, and occasionally gave me what I thought were ignorant ideas that infuriated me. She meant well, but could not seem to understand me, and often seemed angry or disgusted with me when I confessed that I had spent more money. On my own, I hungrily devoured books about addiction, trials, depression and anxiety, as well as books on positive thinking. My counselor suggested that I think of my addiction, as well as of my depression and anxiety, as

78

demons that possessed my body. I prayed desperately for a cure, for help finding my dream job, and became very close to God during these years in my life.

Chapter 7: Fasting & Journaling

At this point in time I had neither concluded nor convinced myself that the use of my credit cards was a sin. I was an adult, it was my choice, and how else was I supposed to pay for day-to-day items that I needed? Interestingly enough, I admit now that I would not hesitate to charge items such as clothes, shoes, or new makeup and lingerie on my credit cards. It was expenses like gas and groceries, car repairs and allergy medicine that actually devastated me to charge. Many times I either did without, but more often I ended up using cash my mom had given me to pay my bills to purchase items that at that time did not give me a fix. An oil change, toothpaste, deodorant, and sunscreen --- it was out of the question or with some resentment that I used my credit cards for these things. I continued my compulsive habit of buying overly expensive gifts for friends and family with my credit cards. I see now that my pride would not permit me to face the fact that I was really

80

in no position to be buying gifts for anyone, including for myself.

I look back now and I think about how irresponsible my spending was, and how extremely grateful I was to my mom for the money she supplied to keep my life going. Obviously a large part of me that I would have liked to deny existed took for granted that she would continue to take responsibility for my bills and for my everyday needs. Also, the more I was actually lacking and depriving myself in the actual basic needs area of my life, the more frantic and deprived I felt. And then the more frantic and deprived I felt, the more often I added new things to my wardrobe to feel reassured that everything was okay.

My counselor urged me each week to live within my means. The main problem was that I had zero means, as I was still unemployed. Also, since before my teens, I'd had a steady supply of cash by stealing from my parents, and then moved right from that into using credit cards. It occurs to me at this very moment ---- I had never, since being old enough to spend money, lived within my means! It was painfully humiliating to ask my mom for a check every six weeks, and her understandably increasingly angry and frustrated reaction caused incredible stress for me each time I needed to work up the courage to approach her. Out of desperation I sold some of my furniture to an auctioneer, for a percentage far less than what I paid for it. And – big surprise - I still have the original debt from the very same furniture purchases, when I no longer even own the items! It seemed that nothing I attempted was profitable. Anything I did manage to earn was just a tiny drop into the gigantic bucket that was my debt. Unfortunately and foolishly, I had the same view when it came to my spending. What, honestly, did a $50 purchase matter at a point when I was already $25,000 in debt????

Every dollar mattered, my counselor insisted. She challenged me to one month without spending. No new clothes or eating out. No buying extras or back-ups of toiletries. Since my mom paid for groceries, I didn't need to spend there, either. I asked, but wasn't even permitted to buy second-hand from a garage sale or thrift store. A month seemed to be unthinkable!! I had always felt so accomplished whenever I had made it through several days without a purchase. But I was in counseling for help, I reasoned. I didn't believe that the month-long shopping fast was necessary.

Inside I was panicked! What about all of the beautiful things out there in the stores and online, with limited inventories??? My size was sure to sell out! I was instructed to avoid temptation and not to visit online shops or physical stores. This is the very first time it had occurred to me not to go to a store when I didn't *need* anything. Window shopping was supposed to be such a

83

charming activity, and what could it hurt to look?? It *always* hurt me to look! I inevitably became fixated on one or more items. These became stuck in my head and then day after day they were built up to such a life-or-death status ---- life literally could not go on if I did not acquire the item, and through any wasteful or ridiculous means possible.

I was terrified of the deep depression I knew I would sink into if I did not pacify the monster inside of me with shopping. And ever since I was a young girl it was drilled into my head that it was not normal to be sad – "***Smile, did someone die?***" or "*Why are you so quiet, does the cat have your tongue???*" I had so much built-up anger and sadness that I had stopped allowing myself to feel because it made people wonder about me in the wrong way, and I honestly preferred that they not wonder about me at all. If you are quiet or look sad because you're deep in thought, as I usually was, then something must be wrong! My

84

response to teachers and family, and eventually to employers, was to bury the parts of me that they interpreted as disturbing. The burden over the course of three decades became so great that I had to restlessly keep moving on to another job, to new and different material things, music unusual enough that no one else around me had ever heard of it, and then also my various name changes. I could not allow anyone to discover who I really was, as I knew by then that they wouldn't like it. After all, the one person who I had allowed to get close to me had betrayed me and abandoned me. No, I needed the shopping for all of these reasons that I was not yet ready to admit to myself.

I gritted my teeth and accepted my counselor's 30-day challenge. I made a sincere promise to a silent God that I would not use my credit cards. I wrote out my pact, signed and sealed it into an envelope, along with all of my precious plastic friends. This tactic would only serve to prevent me from shopping in stores, as I had most of my credit card numbers memorized, and was capable of placing an online order in an expert sixty seconds. I had all kinds of reasons for not actually closing my credit card accounts. I believed that I needed them in case of an emergency. More often than not, a new pair of shoes was the only emergency. I was afraid that closing my accounts would negatively affect my credit score. Also, in those days, closing a credit card was a major hassle, and almost guaranteed a long discussion with multiple people, intrusive questioning, and "accidently" having my call disconnected. My pulse raced with the effort of it, and I was always left with feelings of guilt. Several times I was assured that my account would be closed, only to receive a notice in the mail weeks later congratulating me on a larger credit limit. I can only assume that the credit card employees were penalized when an account was closed.

However, none of this was a legitimate excuse for overspending.

Although I was unemployed, I regularly received new credit card offers, and transferred over my balances with interest onto zero percent interest cards. Almost every new card came with an incentive to make a purchase; usually a fifty or one hundred dollar gift card. This was impossible for me to turn down, and it was a tradition of mine to reward myself for acquiring a new credit card by allowing myself a single purchase. This purchase, I deceitfully convinced myself, would be my *only* purchase on the new card.

From day one of my thirty-day no-spending challenge, I decided to keep an anti-shopping journal, or a log of my emotional distress and mood swings as I dealt with the deprivation. The following is a portion of my journal, demonstrating the ups and downs and obsessive thought

87

patterns that are to be anticipated when withdrawing from an activity that you are relying on to keep yourself stable.

2005   ***Unshopping Journal***

8/9   I had been doing much better at restricting my shopping. But, due to the loss of a terrific and much-needed job opportunity, I slipped into the depths of despair. I mistakenly believed that I had dealt with the disappointment by crying, praying, feeling the appropriate emotions in a healthy and normal way. Sadly, a shopping craze took over me like a wild-fire, blazing through me at all hours and for days. I used (abused) a new credit card that I had just received to use for balance transfers only. One shoe purchase led to a few more purchases as I became more depressed, and then yesterday I spent a few hundred more. Now today, after one final purchase, I have sealed my 2 useable cards into an envelope for one month. I am determined, with God's support, not to use these credit cards for a month with the exception of face wash and exfoliant. I want to be guided by common sense, not by my moods. I want to trust God with my wardrobe and my debt for at least a month, and see what happens. Healing? Shopping binge???

7PM   Already much of the day has passed, and I'm feeling good, if scared about my decision. I don't want to fail. I want to practice a lot of thought-blocking, rather than to plan for my shopping in one month's time, which could create a binge. And Mom trusts me, which makes me sad but relieved. She doesn't know that I still have a problem, which makes it even more important to give up my obsession and take another chance – challenge to be healed this month. This is truly important to me, and I hope a job will follow. I don't want to mess up my future any more than I already have. It's not too late. This isn't even the end of day one and I've already had to thought-block quite a bit. I want to change my thought pattern.

89

8/10   I had a strong temptation this morning to extend the shopping just one more day and buy the $200 Banana Republic pink velvet jacket. And then I thought, "No, that wouldn't be trusting God, and it would make me have everything I want before I stop shopping – just as bad as a binge after this month is over. Maybe some good will come of this....maybe I'll end up with a good job because I am making a new leap of faith to trust God". And then in the afternoon I had a temptation just to look at the jacket online. I did not. I believed that the urge or mood would pass, and it did. A month is really not too long of a time for anyone, except for me!! Lots of continual thought-blocking all day, just when I would prepare to start daydreaming about the pink jacket or the outlet malls, etc. The scary first day is over.

8/11   I had counseling today, and my discussion of this new pact not to shop for a while dominated our discussion. Unless there is a void in my life created by the lack of shopping, God will not be able to fill it. This is my newest conclusion that I have to let go first. Also, at my counselor's suggestion, and based on her personal experience and Jesus' 40-day fast in the Bible, I am going to fast from shopping, looking at online shopping sites and catalogues, and thinking of shopping for 40 days, rather than 30. The idea initially scared me, but I am giving up this comforting habit to reveal the pain and the void and because I am serious this time about being healed of my addiction. Today I feel comforted by my decision. And then, in 40 days, I will shop with a budget and then only once a month to not allow things to grow out of control.

8/12   So depressed. Not thinking about shopping is difficult, and I miss the boost it gives me during the day. Bills and another rejection letter from the terrific job opportunity really hurt and agitated me. I don't feel like shopping right now, but I am just depressed about my unemployed state. Stress about finances!! Thoughts of shopping usually make me feel better. I feel weird, closed off from part of my brain without thinking of shopping.

8PM I finished reading my addiction book, and I believe it has changed my view. I can go through with this and I am bravely committing all of my life to God now, not excluding shopping, as before. I truly believe in a big way that I will be blessed after this commitment, if I stay with it after my shopping trial. I <u>will!</u> I am looking forward to my new life.

8/26   I stopped even keeping track of the days until the 40 are over. I've been throwing out the fall catalogues, but looking at fashion magazines. Strangely, I don't have any real temptations. I have to thought-block to keep from planning my next shopping trip, but I really don't know what I am missing! I will be able to spend money again without getting into more debt. My dilemma now is how much to budget myself at the end of each month. Is $200 *unreasonable?? Should I not shop at all until I am employed again? I am satisfied with my wardrobe since I do not keep seeing things I want. But at the same time, I feel it's a worthy investment to maintain my wardrobe during this time. What about $100, or $150?? I'll just have to pray for guidance. I haven't noticed any guidance so far, but that doesn't mean I'm not being guided. I did purchase an exfoliant because I will run out in a month and it was free shipping. Also, a few supplies at the fabric store for some creative projects, which I concluded are healthy for me to be involved in.*

9/4   I still must be clinging to my wardrobe for safety - - protection from the world as I insist that I must stay fashionable and current at all costs. In my mind I need to invest a bit each month to replace worn out lingerie and add a couple of pieces so that my wardrobe will not be depleted and I will not find myself facing an inevitable binge when I do find my job. Is this the truth or another

93

excuse to hide my need? I keep reanalyzing it to make

sure. Morally, I will still be sneaking around and hiding

things – sure signs of an addiction. It's also my way of

maintaining some independence during this time of living

with my mom, I guess.

11/13   It has been several months since I recorded my

shopping habits in here. I made it through the first 40-day

fast, but just barely. I went to the Fairfield mall on the

very next day, staying within my budget. I put back a

marvelous pair of boots and a pile of other things at TJ

Maxx – just in time! I want to trust that there are more

fabulous boots in my future when I have an income. So,

after this shopping trip, I faced over-stimulation from my

birthday, then the flea market, and then shopping in

Columbus. Then two more trips to TJ Maxx to buy winter

clothes to wear around the house. I tried to fast

immediately again, but there were too many opportunities

at once, and I got back into the addiction/excitement mode.

94

There was a shoe purchase online. With this I delayed my next shopping trip by a week, and also reduced it by $100. There were Hello Kitty purchases, and a visit to the Dayton mall, taking along a credit card for a just-in-case peek in Forever 21. Then last week I ordered two more pairs of shoes, an eyeshadow (oh, I forgot, perfume from Sephora to get a 12-piece gift!) 2 CDs, and some jewelry supplies. I sound very out of control. Oddly, the only burning craving I experienced was for a velvet jacket and an eyeshadow quad which I resisted but did not buy. I felt bored and rebellious when I made all of these purchases. So, Friday night, after ordering shoes and an eyeshadow, I am spending the weekend alone. I opened up to God about everything, my pain, lack of control, and made a list of reasons why I shop:

*To be fashionable

*To replace worn-out items

*Thrill of something new to move me away from the past; boredom

*Achieve unattainable image

*Put all of my creativity into an ensemble

*Numb pain, boredom, and generally upset feelings

Instead of killing myself with guilt, I also focused on all of the positive ways I've healed towards shopping, and the ways I've resisted or made better choices. Focusing on the positive, I believe, will be my way out and avoid casting me into a doomed mood of hopelessness. The ways I can see that I've healed are:

*More positive thinking, outlook

*Being grateful for what I have

*Turned down Victoria's Secret order

*Turned down gold and black shoes

*Turned down velvet jacket

*Bought inexpensive face wash

*Completed 45-day fast

*Bought less expensive eyeshadow

*Didn't take credit card with me everywhere

*Bought Mom a sweatshirt, and didn't get one for myself

So, although it sounds stupid, I finished out the weekend with a trip to the outlet malls. I practiced restraint and considered giving my credit card to my counselor, but this would not prevent me from getting out of control when I have a job again. I somehow lost my motivation last month. Scary. I spent a lot! I guess I am not one of those people who are miraculously and immediately healed from addiction. So I messed up after a successful 40-day fast. I
97

now have a success to refer back to. I am working on appreciating what I have and being more creative when I am bored instead of shopping.

11/14   Up and down mood swings since yesterday. I got the mail from Saturday, and of course there was a credit card bill in it. I had somehow gone over my limit by about $100. So with the fee, my minimum payment is $243!!! Panic!!! I closed my account and they might take away the extra fee after I am under my credit limit. I have decided to close all of my accounts but one. I cried and prayed all day, truly faced with the horror of my addiction. Stealing even briefly crossed my mind! I don't know why it seemed never to have occurred to me before to close my accounts. A very scary prospect. I scrambled around trying to do an emergency balance transfer this morning, and then decided to use my credit card for groceries and use the cash Mom gives me for groceries to pay my bill. I'm desperate, and didn't know what else to do!! I made two

98

purchases today in a hurry, wanting to hoard if this is my
last chance. If this works out, I have just barely quit while
I am ahead. It took some major scheming, on the brink of
dishonesty. I'm ashamed!! So cutting off my supply is the
only solution. I'm also relieved. Now I'll get somewhere.
What prevented me from closing accounts before? So now,
whatever my debt has risen to in the last 6 weeks, it will
begin to creep down, and I can feel relief and be more
honest and open. It will be more possible for me to have a
job and make it on my own again. I have really avoided
praying today because of my shame. No more sprees!
Good, because I am worn out!

11/30/05   Well, four accounts are closed, and then I
faced temptation again by a raised credit limit on my one
remaining card. So I have ordered makeup twice. But I
also sealed a promise to God not to by GoSmile tooth
whitener or purchase anything from Sephora to get the
new 9-piece gift. I am aware that there will always be one

99

more last thing to purchase before I can be content. I noticed that my mind seems to get bored and even craves the temptation of a catalogue or a website. Knowing the danger of finding something that I have to have is exciting! A hunt! Bringing new things home to my apartment and putting them away always felt so soothing and satisfying!

12/5/05   I had a very rough day on Friday – depressing – something bothering me inside and tempting me to shop to feel better. Instead, I ended up crying over Alan that evening. But I did not buy anything. I did a lot of scanning of things online on Sunday. I did make an $80 purchase on Gloss.com today. The reason behind it – boredom and indifference. I was actually (and still am) convinced that I needed the things that I bought. How long before I can shop without guilt? How do I find balance? My guilt is stronger than it ever was, and it is often too painful to make a purchase. I am grateful for this. Otherwise, I feel lost today! The longer I stay here,

the more debt I get into, whether I'm shopping or not. I
want to work!

12/9/05   A trip to Columbus, a coat and jewelry supply
order, along with the groceries on my last credit card
have, to my strange relief, take me close to my limit. So
now, if I have any intention of shopping in January, I
cannot shop for a month. So, so happy and relieved. I
want to try and accomplish peace and quiet inside so that I
can heal a bit. It took some shopping to hit this
breakthrough, but I'm okay with it!

12/11/05   During the last couple of days I have been
semi-panicked and frightened about not having the means
or the credit power to shop. I think of all of the things that
I wish I had bought or that I may have to do without. But
then I am curious, too, to see just how bad it will be, and if
fashionable things and ideas will come into my life with
little effort. Just how long will it be before I have an

income again? And will I experience logic and healing?
I'll be able to look Mom calmly in the eye a little more
comfortably, I suspect.

2/26/06   Nothing too bad to report since the last time I
wrote in here. I have been forced to stick with the budget
of one small credit card each month. With the exception of
the new credit card I opened for a balance transfer. I did
allow myself an extra $150 on that new card before I did
the balance transfer. The old me would have spent $400
in no time at all! But I had the feeling afterwards of
someone who ate too much dessert. So I can tell I've made
some progress. Also, I noticed that even though I've spent
less over the past few months, it is no less or more painful
than spending $600 in a month's time. I still crave
shopping either way, but my guilt is less. Is it more
stressful to have plenty of money and lose it or to not have
any money at all and contribute to someone else losing it?

3/5/06   I got my newest credit card in the mail for a

balance transfer. I'm going to make a purchase, also, in

order to get a $100 gift card. So I am inwardly buzzing

with shopping excitement. Shopping is something sweet to

get me through life. I long for some fulfillment other than

shopping. Shopping and fashion are all about creating an

image, manipulating my outward appearance to coincide

with who I happen to be on the inside.

Rereading my shopping journal, I can easily conclude that

I still had a lot of issues with defining needs and wants.

But the shopping fast of one month became forty days and

was, for the most part, successful. Even though I binge-

shopped afterwards, I had learned some valuable skills.

Thought-blocking and avoiding temptation became

important tools for me. Once the fast was over and the

compulsive shopping returned, attempting to focus on

positive progress I had made was imperative. For me,

there would obviously be no quick cure.

103

I believed from what I had read and researched about addiction that by successfully making it through my shopping fast, I had constructed some tiny bridges within my brain. These bridges were a foundation of healthy patterns and were pointed in the right direction. A decade of abusing money and burying negative emotions by spending had worn away a deep riverbed of habitual behavior. I was confident that if I persisted in improving that I could eventually re-route the river of repeated negative and unhealthy behavior and dry up my addiction. It was in this same spirit that my counselor encouraged me to fast from food one day a week. I was reluctant, since I am hypoglycemic, but gave it a very good try. Once a week I would have only the bare minimum – a cracker or tea once an hour, or occasionally vegetable juice or broth. Nothing more. My weekly fast was physically and mentally challenging. But the several months of one day a week fasting made me stop and think about hunger.

104

Hunger was the main reason I wanted to eat, of course, when I fasted. But there was a void created in my life from *not* eating as well as from *not* shopping. Other reasons for my cravings were exposed, but only when I slowed down enough to question myself. My hunger in itself could be translated into hunger for shopping, hunger for food, or hunger for companionship or hunger for a relief from emotional pain. Unfortunately it was too easy to channel all of my hunger into one area, if it was not being sufficiently satisfied in another area. This was an easier and almost automatic solution than it would be to try to get to the origin of the appetite in the first place. I had to learn to question myself about *why* I was eating and *why* was I spending?

Most of us grew up in a society where both eating and shopping are treated as entertainment. Eliminating all but the actual *need* as a reason to engage in either activity not only sent me into a panic, but also made me sigh with

105

boredom. I had suddenly gained more intellectual as well as physical time when I cut out any wasteful consumption. Like any addict, although I appreciated these revelations, they were much too much for me to handle. I no longer denied the truth, but I realized it and became casually acquainted with it. Then I pushed it to the back of my mind and continued to live a life of using my credit cards.

Chapter 8: Bankruptcy; to File or Not to File?

Still without a job, during the summer of 2006, I could see no possible way to prevent myself from using credit cards when I had absolutely no income. My days were continually occupied with job searching for full and part-time positions, all over the country, and some even around the world. There were jobs that I was interested in and excited about, but many of the jobs I applied for would simply have brought in a much needed paycheck. Full of despair, and very much ashamed that my mom was paying my bills after all of this time, I decided that by the end of August, if I *still* had not found work, then I would begin the process of filing for bankruptcy.

Bankruptcy!!! I had always, always been determined *not* to see this as an option for myself. I felt that there was no valid reason for me, personally, not to pay off my debt. It might take many years and lots of small payments to accomplish, but this was a responsibility I could not abandon. I did not want to have kids, but I fervently wished to build a career and invest my life in my work. In my mind and in the future, I was single and successful and independent and the type of responsible person who would take care of my own debt, and not turn it over to society. I had been encouraged by friends and acquaintances for years to file for bankruptcy and start fresh. Forget my financial mistakes. Even my mom semi-encouraged this as a way out. Other people suggested that I just stop making my monthly payments; would it really be all that bad to have creditors harassing me? After all, I had nothing to give them, and nothing at all to lose. Except my debt-laden, but otherwise spotless credit report. Oh, and one more thing…. ***my hope for the future and my dream of being a successful business owner.***

My career had been a miserable trial for me up to this point. The one undying piece of me that kept me going to

108

dead-end job after dead-end job, discouraging interview after discouraging interview, despite the even more discouraging rejection letters, was the secret knowledge deep inside of me, *ever* since I was a young girl, that I was going to be a successful business owner one day. Now in my 30's, with evidence pointing in the opposite direction of success, I had to persist in believing that I was closer than ever to my destiny.

I was a misfit --- a very lost creative person who could not seem to find a job that wanted me or suited me, or even that I suited. Something was always missing – a major creative element, room to be promoted, enough salary to even live on --- a job that I actually enjoyed and didn't give me a nervous breakdown or send me to the mall in despair each weekend. My plan was to land either *the* dream job, finally, after so many years, or to work in the graphic design field until I was 40, paying off my debt, and then taking the plunge to start my own business. What exactly this business would be for sure, I had not yet decided. A large part of the assignments for my graphic design classes had revolved around the creation of a fictional company from concept to the end designs. I created "Navare Jewelry". Navare was an ancient kingdom between France and Spain, and I had read quite a bit about its fascinating history. Perhaps this would be the first part of my creative business?? I also dreamed of my own whimsical clothing line – named "Excavation". The apparel would be inspired by a merger of fashion and archaeology. Each piece of clothing would have an interesting trinket or artifact hidden within it. Lastly, a restaurant named "Crème" – for one of my favorite foods – cream! My tiny restaurant would have ultra-rich, small portions, and would be safe for those, like myself, who suffer from food allergies and intolerances. Crème would refrain from using gluten, dairy, and corn in anything on the menu.

So these were my ideas. This dream inside of me would not allow me to give up and file for bankruptcy. And no job had ever come close to fulfilling me the way that I knew my business would. I planned to stop spending so heavily and to gradually pay off my debt, but instead I continued to bury myself in financial crisis, dollar by dollar. No matter how good of a deal I got on anything, as long as I paid by credit card, I knew it would be years before I actually got to the point of paying that particular item off. By that time, it had cost me an absurd amount. I was armed with all of the facts, but I hadn't applied the information to my actual life. When I did find my new job, I vowed that I would actually stop using credit cards.

That August, miraculously enough, I was given a 2-week freelance assignment to work as a photo stylist. The company brought two new employees in on trial, and, much to my dismay, they first hired a girl fresh out of college and with zero experience in the career world. This

111

was a bitter medicine to swallow. Lesson learned – life does not owe you anything, and sometimes success is pure luck! I also soon found out that while I had been job searching for 2 ½ years, the newly hired employee had not even been seriously job searching. She had accidently stumbled across the ad for the position. Nothing could have seemed more heartbreakingly unfair, but by the end of the third week, I was finally hired in alongside of my bossy young coworker.

So very grateful to finally have a job and a paycheck, I hungrily attacked the responsibilities I was given in the studio. I actually finally felt as if I had found a real career where I could learn and quickly be promoted, and my bright and shiny future twinkled in the near distance. My coworker and I started at the very bottom of the barrel. Steaming and ironing for days in the un-air-conditioned back studio and being sent out with long lists to shop for the senior stylists. I came in early, left late, and

112

volunteered to work on weekends. Forty hours just did not seem like enough

As it turned out, a major part of my job was shopping for props, wardrobe, and furniture. While I was out shopping for work in some of my favorite stores, I almost always spotted something that I required for myself. I had a new apartment to furnish, and after finally unpacking the boxes of my belongings after two years, I discovered that my tastes had changed. I disposed of many things that no longer interested me, or that reminded me of life with my ex. And then of course I needed more aesthetically pleasing replacements.

I was a new person, and no longer felt like the name Sakhmet defined me. Veille was the first in a series of inspired names that I used during my years at the photo studio. I felt so much happiness and relief --- too much for me to know how to process. I was absolutely bursting at

113

the seams with creativity, but was bewildered to have shopping cravings brought on by too much happiness! I made a list of all of the things I had been deprived of during my years as Sakhmet. I believed I deserved to be rewarded with these things, and made all of these final purchases on my credit cards before I closed them. If only I had stopped to ask myself....did the Me of the future deserve to have to be stuck with all of the debt from these new items?

I researched and considered doing a debt consolidation program, but my salary wasn't high enough to be able to make the required minimum payments. Next, I attempted to take out a loan from my bank in order to consolidate my $25,000 of credit card debt, but was turned down because of my low income. Perhaps she shouldn't have, but my mom came to the rescue once again. She heroically took out a loan in her name in order to pay off my debt. I was to make payments to her each month, and then when the

114

balance was low enough, I planned to take out my own

loan in order to pay her off. Both my mom and I look back

at this today, and wish that she hadn't come to my rescue.

She had my best interests in mind, but once again, I

escaped the consequences of my addiction.

Chapter 9: A Career in Shopping

I earned a lot of overtime hours during the first four months of my new job, and so I easily used cash for my purchases, rather than credit. I was pleased with myself, and genuinely believed that my addiction was no longer a problem. My bills were paid each month, with something extra left over for a weekly purchase of one or more items. Suddenly, though, the holidays were over and my company began laying people off mere months after hiring in many new employees. My fellow stylists and I were terrified, and each day was a challenge to stay or appear busy. Although there was very little for us to do since we had entered a slow season, it was important to look productive and busy. I was not laid off, but over-time hours were forbidden and I suddenly found myself living paycheck to paycheck, struggling to buy groceries or fuel for my car. My weekly shopping dwindled, but I still could not allow a weekend to pass by without a purchase. I remember wandering through a mall, not finding anything I wanted, and then finally buying a Lancome eyeshadow, just for the sake of pacifying the need to shop. An at-least-once-weekly indulgent purchase was as essential to me as seeing my friends, or more extremely, buying groceries. It was called to my attention again by the ridiculous severity of the situation that I still had a problem – despite the fact that I was spending cash, and not incurring new debt.

My mom saw my struggles, and not my addiction. She advised me to stop making payments to her on the loan, and instead instructed me to make larger payments on my student loan, which was around $12,000. I had every intention of doing this, and for the first few months I followed through. But my money was so tight that I ended up paying very little extra on my student loan and instead kept the money to make my day-to-day life a bit less stressful and a little more fun. It was nice to be able to eat

117

out occasionally, to get daily coffee drinks, and to have gas money to be able to meet up with friends, who were all located quite a distance from my apartment. Before spring was over, we were free to work overtime again, and I threw myself into my newly acquired food-styling responsibilities.

I was having so much fun learning, building my portfolio, and buying new clothes and shoes. Coworkers at every job have commented to me that they never saw me wearing the same thing twice. Well, they must not have been looking closely enough, as I most certainly did wear the same thing more than once, just not usually in the same way. It was *not* a good week for me if I didn't have at least one new thing to wear. By visiting thrift stores on a regular basis, I was often able to find several used articles of clothing for the price of one item from a retail store that sold new merchandise.

No matter how stressful or exciting my work was, the highlight of my day was each evening when I would spend time putting together my outfit for the following day, going along with my mood or *who* I was feeling like. It set each work day off to a very good start as long as I was excited about what I was wearing. But was that all there was to my life besides work? I look back, and it seems like it. I must have felt empty inside, but clearly I was filling the void with material things.

By mid-summer I was given the assignment that I had been begging my bosses for – the position as the main stylist for my company's new account with Joann Fabric and Crafts. I had quickly grown bored with food styling and had been eager to move on to something new. And spending two entire work days styling a stack of towels or a bed was something I just didn't have the patience for. My favorite producer had confessed to me that there were never going to be any promotions available in the

119

company beyond just a basic prop stylist. This, of course, devastated me, and I hoped to prove him wrong.

My appetite for new responsibilities was insatiable, and although my new promotion did not involve a raise, I eagerly delved into my pile of work. My new position gave me lots of extra hours and the independence to organize my days as I chose. I spent a great deal of time out of the studio shopping for props, and came in early, left late, and worked many weekends on my own. Depending on the sets that would be photographed each week, I almost always had a three or four page list of items to buy. I knew the contents of most of Columbus' retail stores by heart, and made my regular rounds of the clothing stores where I was sure to find something for myself. My purchases added up, and I grew accustomed to larger paychecks. I once worked sixty days straight without a day off, and can remember feeling very lonely and sort of emotionally bankrupt. This is how I had always envisioned my career – lots of work and extra money to buy the things that would keep me happy. I didn't have much time for friends and family, but I became an obedient slave to work and shopping.

My activities kept me so busy that I didn't have time to feel my usual pain. I was so constantly stimulated by purchases that the years of accumulated sadness didn't have the opportunity to touch me. Assuming my promotion always kept me so out of touch with reality, I knew that years, like the past months, would pass by quickly. I had learned what I was capable of, and it gave me the confidence to want more. A persistent question twinkled like a bright star in the back of my mind, requiring my attention. *When*, when would be the time to pursue my big dream??? Had I found it yet? My exhausting schedule certainly left no time for anything else.

121

I pondered my life and my destiny, and then my answer was delivered when it all came crashing down around me. The busy season ended and we eased our way into the slow season. Layoffs occurred at a maddening pace, and newly hired employees were let go without a care. My company lost several significant accounts, and so on Fridays, paranoia penetrated every cubicle. Rumors circulated about who would be the next to go. Like employees at many companies during the recession, those of us who remained were forced to take an unpaid day off each week for eight weeks. Perhaps worst of all for the studio, my boss returned from a three-month leave of absence and was afraid of her own loss of power. She stopped at nothing to secure her position, although her absence had only made the studio more efficient. My boss did not appreciate my adventurous sense of responsibility, or the fact that I had begun designing some of the sets. Set styling was the next big goal for me. While my boss was

122

away, I had been able to assume more and more responsibility, and was very well organized at keeping track of all of the sets, the dates, the props, and the models' sizes. My boss had returned to the studio to find herself no longer needed. Her secret was out for all to see– the photographers and stylists teamed up to do her job more efficiently than she could ever do. It was the general opinion that she could be laid off and the studio would run more smoothly and profitably without her. Her answer to this was to take away all promotions and responsibilities earned while she was away. I found myself demoted, and had every ounce of creativity sucked right out of my job. I went from having the glorious freedom of organizing all of the Joann's photo shoots straight back to the infuriating frustration of working on the dullest of sets.

I have never been someone who liked to sit still for very long. In fact, this book was written in lots of small sessions because of this fact. My boss took away everything that I loved about my job and was good at, and deliberately forced me onto assignments that would showcase my inability to work on low-energy and tedious projects. Try as I might, I just could not accept the fact that my career was going in reverse. From then on each work day became an eight hour punishment.

I now had three day weekends to contend with, and little or no money to shop with. My paychecks were smaller, and I struggled once more to pay my bills. If only I had thought to save a little money when overtime hours had been abundant. I took refuge at my mom's house each weekend in order to job search and save money on groceries. Somehow, when I had started the photo styling job, a part of me knew that I would only be with the company for two years. But it seemed so heart-wrenchingly unjust!! This job was the closest that I had come to a real career, and it had been one that allowed me to use some of my creativity. But I just wasn't earning

124

enough money. By now, everyone in my social group had an income that far surpassed mine, and I felt left behind. I hoped with all of my heart that this job which had started out so well, was merely another trial that would soon come to an end. Wanting the misery of the experience to serve a greater purpose, I focused on learning whatever I could about patience, hope, a positive attitude, and the prevalence of good over evil.

It seemed that my entire life since college had been one big job search full of trial and error. _All_ that seemed to soothe me was shopping. I had a truly deep relationship with God during this time, or there is absolutely no way that I could have endured the immense stress of the studio. But I certainly hadn't reached a level of relying on Him, rather than on material things.

By early spring I was officially reprimanded for one thing or another at work on a weekly basis. My boss made regular attacks on anyone she believed to be her competition, and especially on anyone who dared to expose her lies. *Never* had I met someone who was such a blatant fraud. None of the rest of us had the character to stoop to her level, which was something she obviously counted on. Those who dared to stand up for what was right paid dearly with the safety of our jobs.

I did not want this to be my battle. I did not want to remain in that position any longer and become another unhappy person with an unfulfilling job who takes out her own life's disappointments on those who are unfortunate enough to be under her influence. My escape, therefore, was all that consumed me. It was around this time that I counted out the work days remaining until I would have been with the company for exactly two years. I determined and dared to *believe* with everything inside of me that I would be free by that date. Each day began with my announcement to a few coworkers of how many days I

126

had remaining to work there. It started out at an unbelievable 160 days. I clung to my countdown and tried to have a positive attitude. Shamefully, I also clung to my new credit card, and to the purchases I made to get me through the weeks ahead.

I spent any extra cash I had, and whenever a week had been worse than usual, I allowed myself an extra purchase with the credit card. My credit card use wasn't nearly as extreme as it had been during my unemployed years, but just the fact that I had dared venture into that territory again after my mom had so generously taken out a loan to cover my other credit card debt displayed the fact that I still had a serious problem. Didn't I ever learn from my mistakes? How could I betray my mom??? And what would have to occur in order for me to take my debt and my spending seriously? The thing was, I always had taken my spending seriously, for years and years, but I could not find a solution or a way to stop no matter what I tried.

127

My guilt, though not haunting as it once had been, still clung to me like a shadow. I could not identify for sure or admit that much of my guilt came with my shopping and my credit card use. It had a snowball effect, as I could not endure the accusing tone of my thoughts, and lonely weekends once again drove me to the mall, a thrift store, or the always dangerous Target. If I was occupied with friends, a favorite activity was usually to hunt for the next best thing to add to our wardrobes. I absolutely resented the fact that I was still living paycheck to paycheck, so close to losing my job, and, in reality couldn't afford to keep up with my friends without using a credit card. For these days, if I worked extra hours early the week, I was forced to take off unpaid time later in the week. I wish that a part of me would have realized at the time all that I was so fortunate to have....my own place to live, a car, a job, enough money for food, health insurance....the list goes on and on, but I was too preoccupied with comparing my life and my income with those around me.

It was midsummer, 2008. My job search was still proving to be fruitless, but I continued to pray and to believe for the sake of my sanity that I would find a job by the end of my two year anniversary count-down. Skeptics were all around me, but I would not be discouraged – at least not permanently. I decided to change my approach, and instead applying for large quantities of jobs, focus on a single company that I admired, and the company that I most believed had the dream job I had been waiting for and searching for, for more than a decade.

How many hundreds of resumes and cover letters and hopes and pleas had I sent out since my college graduation?? How many job applications had I filled out, and how many heart-breaking interviews had I been on, only to receive rejection after rejection? I searched for my dream job, for my career, with the sincere angst and desperation that some people search and wait for their soul mates to come along. Why had I continued to sabotage myself by accruing more and more debt? Somehow, in my mind, my dream career and the end of my shopping addiction went hand-in-hand. Only something so fulfilling and so worthwhile would be valuable and powerful enough to eclipse my addiction. So far in my life I had tried as hard as I knew how to bravely let go of my addiction and to heal, but obviously nothing else had been important enough yet for me to allow this to take place. I was so driven, almost to the point of madness, a friend had once warned me. I *wanted* to give up, to be satisfied with any job that came my way and paid the bills, but I did not seem to be capable of giving up. It seemed that whenever I let go and permitted myself an opportunity to give up my dream then my mind would be set free to wander. All of the discouragement over my current situation would be released, and I would gradually feel reinvigorated and full of fresh ideas about my career and a new life, without ever intending to. It was the natural course of my thought life that never allowed me to give up. I could not help but believe that God was behind this, as it always circled back around to feel again like my true purpose in life.

Chapter 10: The Allure of the Big Dream

I had hand-sewn an eye-catching resume out of pieces of colorful origami paper and vellum. I then carefully assembled a few of the most captivating antique and vintage trinkets that I could find into a perfect little box, along with my most honest and heartfelt cover letter ever. Full of passion, I inserted several photos from my styling portfolio, and prepared my package of creativity and enthusiasm to be mailed to the Anthropologie and Urban Outfitters headquarters in Philadelphia. Strangely and frustratingly, I could not find an address or even a contact name to mail my package to. After a couple of hours of extensive online research, I called the local Anthropologie store for help. I explained my mission, but no one in the store could find the address for their home office anywhere, either. I was, however, invited to bring my portfolio into the store and interview for the Apparel

132

Department Manager position. *Really*??? It seemed too good to be true, and possibly meant to be. I not only dropped off my resume that very same weekend, but also picked up a few new pieces of clothing for the interviews that I was confident would take place.

A couple of weeks and many calls to the store later, I had my first interview at Anthropologie. The apparel department manager position, I was told, was the second most powerful in the store. I would be in control of all of the clothing and accessories, in addition to having the privilege of changing all of the window mannequins on a weekly basis. The little bit of customer service involved would not bother me in the least, I assured my interviewer, while I quietly wondered about it myself. Best of all, this was a company that believed in promoting from within. I could move up the ranks quickly and relocate to the home office within a few years. The job I *really* wanted was the visual merchandising position, but it had been filled just

133

the week before. There was an artist on staff full-time, and the managers were expected to treat the store as if it were their own small business. The perfect environment in which to learn about running my own business someday, I thought! As for any worries over the customer service responsibilities that had driven me mad just years before, I convinced myself that my antisocial nature would be tamed by all of the creativity that I would soon be immersed in.

I was called in for a second interview with Anthropologie– this time with the district manager. My appointment occurred during an important photo shoot on which I was the main stylist, and so I faked a migraine, and let another stylist and a producer in on the secret so that they would cover for me while I made my escape. The very next week I had the privilege of turning in my two week notice to my very shocked boss. She had been looking forward to laying me off right after the busy season, I had heard, and words

134

cannot describe the look of sad defeat on her face. It was with extreme gratification that I realized my last day at the studio was on the exact date of my two-year anniversary! My mysterious countdown of days had been in sync with my gut instinct, as well as with God's plan for me. I had hoped and wished and prayed and job searched in impossibly large quantities towards this triumph.

My mind spun at a dizzying speed during the two weeks before I began what was to at long last be the career I had hungrily pursued for ten years. It was strange – my boss almost seemed afraid of me now, and began treating me with the respect one might give to a sorceress, and from a refreshing distance. What a victory it was to have obvious proof that I was being looked after by someone greater than myself!! It was astonishing to believe that all it took was for me to identify the actual company where I could find my dream job opportunity, and my life would begin anew. All of the anxiety and panic and worries evaporated as if they had never been, and I was relieved to understand that if I took a simple, calm, and common sense approach to my life and kept my eyes on God, I would stay on the right path.

Just as I had when I had started my job as a stylist, or any new job, for that matter, I evaluated my wardrobe and concluded with alarm that it was lacking. So then the credit card that had been in semi-hibernation made itself useful by buying eight new pairs of shoes and boots, in preparation for standing on my feet all day. For clothing, I would wait until I had my forty percent off discount, which, -gasp! - could also be used at Urban Outfitters and Free People. This was my true career, and I was determined not to splurge. Good things were just ahead. After all, I lived about 45 minutes away from my new workplace, and would need to move closer when my lease expired in two months. A move is always costly, and there would undoubtedly be new household items to buy. My new starting salary wasn't any higher than what I made at the studio, and so I had to be very careful how I spent my earnings. I couldn't jeopardize the successful future that was now close enough to feel real.

My first nerve-wracking day arrived, and I still could not fathom that this beautiful store, full of the most sought-after treasures, was to be my new workplace. I was frozen with terror and awe, and spent the first half of the day safely filling out paperwork in the tiny back office. There were so many manuals to read, and so many new rules to memorize and follow. It really struck me as odd right away that a company as free and creative as Anthropologie was would be so very strict and particular about everything. There was a mind-boggling amount of paperwork that had to be completed for my departments daily and weekly, and it was with great relief when I went out on the sales floor for the second half of the day. I was prepared to settle in and make myself at home.

Customer service was the part of my new job that I embraced with open but wary arms. As an introverted person, I inwardly cringe each time I meet someone new. I wanted to learn customer service in a way that I had never attempted in any of my past retail jobs. Besides, I reasoned, I could automatically look at all of the customers as my friends, since we had our love of Anthropologie in common. I felt so fortunate to have been hired by such an artistic and open-minded company! And so long as I continued to learn, I hoped to never grow bored.

It was with great anticipation on my second day of the new job that I met my assistant. She had wanted my position, I knew, but had a lack of sophistication and style. She looked anything but Anthropologie, and didn't appear to be a dedicated follower of fashion. I needed her to be on my side, and to teach me what she had learned in the two months since she started working there, uncomfortable though it might be. Besides, I had just come out of a war

138

zone, and under no circumstances wanted to contribute to anyone else's misery the way that my boss had contributed to mine. I was determined, above all else, to treat anyone working under me with kindness and understanding.

I was soon confronted with the obvious realization that it takes both people to want to get along with each other. My assistant not only insisted to me that she was indeed *not* a new employee, but was apparently a seasoned expert after only eight weeks! She contradicted me at every turn, disagreed with my suggestions, and bombarded me with orders. She put on a pleasant face when other managers were around, but her hostility was revealed as soon as she and I were alone working together again.

So then, I was excited to meet the visual merchandiser, who I knew I would be working with as closely as my assistant. Without going into too much detail, I quickly realized that she, too, was going to be next to impossible to get along with, with her monosyllabic answers to my questions, and twelve hour workdays without a lunch break. In her opinion, my opinion was not a valid one. The visual manager, just like my old boss at the studio, felt the need to control and correct my point of view so that in the end, the only right way was her way. The problem was, that if this job was to be the fulfilling job that it was meant to be, I had to have the creative authority that was promised to me when I was offered the job. I did not need another controlling art director in my life, as I had creatively matured to a point that it was essential to me to follow my own vision. What it was that made something beautiful and aesthetically pleasing was a matter of opinion, and I had the confidence to believe in the beauty that I was capable of creating. I was no longer capable of pretending to follow a creative vision that I did not believe in.

140

One week into the job, I was still looking for things to love and to enjoy. By the end of week two, it was apparent that my main 50-hour a week job was customer service and managing the employees. There was not even a spare moment to begin changing mannequins and displays and bulletin boards and putting out new merchandise and all of the other dozens of tasks and projects and competitions that poured in from the home office. I quickly learned that the Anthropologie store had a rapid turnover rate for managers who were terribly overworked and disgracefully underpaid. A part-time employee who had worked there for ten years confessed that she had seen dozens of girl hired in, only to leave broken-down, with dreams crushed. She finally quit in protest over the injustice of overworked managers.

There was no possible way to end my shift after eight hours, as the other responsibilities and assignments given to me by the visual manager had only begun. At the end

141

of week two I had not had time to see my friends, and I realized I seldom would. Working weekends, there would never be a chance to drive to Piqua to spend time with my family. If I thought I had been lonely before this job, I had been mistaken. I could never have a pet, or be home at a decent time to take my soothing daily walks. The little things in life that I loved and that meant something to me would all evaporate with this new job. If I was going to work this hard for this many hours with no creative fulfillment, shouldn't I instead decide to work this hard on something I cared about – which was my future business? The one thing I had to lean on with this new job was shopping. That was it! My dependency could only grow greater. How could I face the fact that the only thing I enjoyed about my new job was the things we sold? This was not enough.

My assistant continued to put on a kind front for the other managers, and was as difficult as she could be when it was

142

just the two of us. I was emotionally exhausted after another 12-hour work day alongside of her, and left the store with a stern scolding from the visuals manager for leaving tasks unfinished. There was no earthly way to complete all of my work, remain sane, sleep, and have any kind of a real life outside of the store. Out of desperation on the long drive home, I wanted to drive my car full speed ahead into the cement wall along the interstate. I felt like a tragic mess! Ten solid years of job searching – for *this!!!*

I saw my life ahead of me; my aspirations to start my own business---the *one major dream* that had fueled all of my attempts to find a fulfilling career. There were two distinct paths right in front of me, each pointing in the opposite direction. One, to tough it out at Anthropologie. I would need to wage war against the visual manager and to ruthlessly put my assistant in her place. I could work my way up the ranks by becoming cold and calculating, by

143

being unkind and competitive the way that so many people climb their way to the top. I had witnessed this, been a victim of it, and knew that I was capable of it – motivated by greed and power. In doing this and pursuing this type of career for myself, my family and friends would slowly fade from my life, as they had when I'd worked long hours at the studio. I would need to become a workaholic, which was very much in my genes, and I could kiss the dream of starting my own business goodbye. Even though I hadn't seemed to make much progress in my career, I had made progress at becoming a better, kinder, and more compassionate person. It had become supremely important to me to treat people well and with respect, and more so with each cruel manager I had had to work with. We all have people at our mercy at some point in our lives, and I couldn't bear the thought of making people miserable for forty hours of every week, since that was the type of manager personality that was expected of me.

144

It was during my next day off that I travelled to my mom's house to partake of her wisdom with long discussions. I put lots of thought and prayer into this major decision, weighing the pros and cons of each. I wanted to make sure that I wasn't just running away from something. I consciously chose happiness and mental health over greed and addiction, and triumphantly turned in my resignation during the next day at work. I agreed to work six more weeks as a manager until my apartment lease ended, but forfeited my responsibilities as department manager, and refused to work more than forty hours each week. I had a lot to plan, and knew from what I felt was the strongest gut instinct that I'd ever experienced – it was now or never --- the time to jump off of a cliff and start my own small business.

The six weeks following were the longest and some of the most miserable in my life. My shopping addiction swelled to titanic proportions, and the only thing that got me

145

through each dreadful day was to buy everything that I wanted. Word soon spread among the employees about my resignation, and everyone chose a side. It was apparent, then, who had only been nice to me because of my position, as they quickly switched loyalties and became inseparable from my assistant. Stories came out of the woodwork about dozens of unhappy managers in the past, just like me. They had been swindled into believing that they had been hired for their creativity and style, but instead had been overworked until they were fortunate enough to make their escape. The clothes and shoes and accessories were like sweet poisons that sedated me and drained me...I had a fever and could not stop buying. And since I had first started the job, whenever I had a day off, I supposed I might as well make the most of it – hoarding and shopping as if my life depended on it. What had ever made me think that I was strong enough to resist my shopping addiction if I went back to a retail career? This

146

job truly would have brought me to utter financial and emotional destruction, and nearly did. I did not know what lay ahead, but suspected reasonably that shopping would not be included for a while. Preparing for famine by feasting must have been my state of mind.

I was terrified at the prospect of being unemployed again and immediately began looking for part-time work near my mom's house. I could not believe that I was volunteering to forfeit my independence and pack up my belongings and move back to the small city of Piqua. I would be away from my friends and away from shopping; isolated from any sort of distraction. A large part of me felt as if I wasn't giving up anything at all, that I may instead be gaining my life back, as in just a very short time, Anthropologie had robbed me of a life and of freedom. This change reminded me of the move I had made when I went back to school and moved to Dayton to escape from major shopping temptation several years

147

before. I needed help with my addiction; that much was for sure. The force of it during this jolting life decision was something I could not ignore. Even if all of my self-doubts taunted me for quitting my job in the unstable economy, it was with absolute certainty that I knew this retail job would destroy me. Watching customers walk out of the store with clothing that I loved, and sometimes selling the last piece in my size, was a torture that made me cringe (or go on a search for something else to satisfy my loss). There was nothing fulfilling to me about my job at Anthropologie except for the shopping. The job was dry and stale and forcefully sociable, which made it the opposite of anything I could enjoy. And my true career was supposed to be the antidote for my addiction. What I needed was something that mattered enough to me to slow down or even stop my shopping long enough to enable me to heal. Not a self-imposed fast that drove me to binge, but something I wanted with every ounce of my being.

148

Something worth making a promise to God – a negotiation – to trust Him with my future – that my bills would be paid – and to guide me into the career that I knew with absolute certainty would fulfill me in a way that shopping never could. I just needed a taste of it to start with, so that I could begin to let go.

Four thousand dollars in eight weeks! The damage had already been done, and still I was not satisfied. I had a phenomenal appetite that was never satiated, even when I was sure I had had enough the day before. The next day I would find a few more things that I had to have before I could think about giving it all up. It would not be easy. But I had to get my wardrobe to a perfect place before the great shopping binge came to an end.

The last day of the false dream job finally arrived. I left with a large bag of merchandise and received a scowl and an eye roll as parting gifts. I spent my final day in

Columbus with friends, shopping as if it was the last time ever. Moving day was sad, and I panicked at all of the intimidating challenges that lay just ahead. My plan was to secure a part-time job as quickly as possible, with enough of a paycheck to pay my monthly bills. I had just enough money from my final paycheck to pay the movers with a bit leftover. At the last moment, I decided to keep my cash, and even paid for part of the move with my credit card. I calculated that I had enough money to pay bills for three weeks, and believed with all of my heart that a part-time job would turn up. In the meantime, I would open an Etsy shop – a popular website that I had discovered where you could easily sell vintage and handmade goods. It cost twenty cents to list an item, and the site charged another small percentage each time an item was sold. To open a shop was free, and this was the perfect, inexpensive way for me to start my small business.

So what would I sell? The answer had come to me obviously and suddenly on that terrifying night when I had been faced with the reality that I could not possibly continue working at Anthropologie. I had created my own jewelry for years from vintage pieces scavenged from flea markets and garage sales. If I did buy new jewelry from a retail store, I typically transformed it into something more unique. I was encouraged by compliments from friends, family, and complete strangers or customers whenever I wore one of my own creations. I also altered and embellished much of the clothing I wore, but a clothing line would be a more expensive and complicated venture. I could start my jewelry business by using items that I already owned. And a small investment each month for pieces and components from flea markets and thrift stores would provide me with all of the supplies I would need to build up my inventory.

The more I thought about it, the more this venture made perfect sense for me to pursue. This was really the only thing related to my interests and natural talents that I had not yet attempted. Years ago, I had sent away for information from a college that offered a degree in jewelry design. I had concluded that it was too expensive, but from then on I had applied for jobs and internships in jewelry stores. I was interested, and wanted to learn more about the industry. As I pondered my new situation a little deeper, I realized that it had a dual purpose. If I was truly passionate about giving this business all I had, I would have no choice but to withdraw from my shopping addiction. If this plan was indeed my sought-after destiny, and, in other words, meant to be, then, despite the horrible economy, I would be able to quickly find a part-time job and be able to pay my monthly bills.

I was willing to take the enormous risk because I had faith in God that He was guiding me in the right direction –

152

especially since I had already been in all of the other directions in some way, shape, or form, since finishing college. I set to work almost frantically, designing a logo and business cards for my new shop. I also applied to masses of local part-time jobs and was quickly hired as a seasonal sales associate at a retail store.

By the end of November 2008, my tiny shop was opened and friends and family members became my first customers. I kept myself as busy as I could by making and photographing new jewelry to build up my inventory, and in learning everything I could about starting a small business and running an online shop. Little did I know that I had some of the most discouraging years of my life ahead of me. But finally, the direction I was taking felt refreshingly very right!

My seasonal retail job was quickly and gladly left in the dust when a friend in Cleveland offered me a freelance assignment alongside of her as a prop stylist for a Super Bowl commercial. The job lasted ten days, and not surprisingly, I found many opportunities to add to my credit card debt. It was the same situation as when I had worked at the studio – I shopped for the job and found plenty of new things for myself. The month of December ended and I was paid well enough for my work on the commercial that I had enough money to pay my bills until my tax refund arrived.

Chapter 11: Trusting God with my Wardrobe...What an Odd Idea!

I want to point out that I was very much aware that I was being irresponsible with money, and also that I urgently needed to put my financial priorities in order if I did not want to lose what was likely a single chance to pursue my fulfilling dream. Beginning with my last paycheck at Anthropologie, and continuing with any income thereafter, I set aside twelve percent of sales and ten percent of paychecks to pass along to someone less fortunate. If I was going to build a successful business, I wanted to start things off in the best way possible. This meant stamping out some of my personal greed, in order to build a very solid foundation for my business. I allowed myself a few clothing purchases with my tax refund, but everything else went into my business for supplies, packaging, labels, and advertising. I hoped that God was taking note of my newly established responsible behavior.

New businesses are built with risks, and I was certainly a risk-taker. By late spring of 2009 my money was dwindling, and jewelry sales were not enough to make ends meet. Out of desperation, I put a $150 online advertisement on my credit card. But no results! I had begun to have a few sales each month from new customers who somehow had found my shop, but the sales were certainly not enough to make much of a dent in my bills. Often, the excitement of having a sale would trigger me to make a purchase. Sad, but true! Perhaps it was the over-stimulation of a happy or exciting event, providing me with the emotion that I was incapable of processing in a normal and healthy way.

Once more, I found myself turning in job applications left and right and was finally hired at a staffing agency. To my great dismay and enormous fear, I was chosen to fill in occasionally at the front desk of a factory. The factory was in a village near Piqua, and the president was an angry

156

tyrant. I appreciated the pay, but I did not want to end up like the employees at the factory. They lived miserable, rough lives, and were extremely poor. Females in the factory were not respected, and the office workers cowered in fear of the one in power. Was this how I would end up if I did not curb my spending and somehow get my business to grow? I was haunted by these thoughts as I made it through my first excruciating week at the factory. There was not a lot to do, and it required me to sit all day, chained to the phone. An angry pair of eyes and ears in the office behind me judged my every word and doubtless my every move. The biggest temptation of all time was the internet access. It kept me busy, and was my constant companion. I am ashamed to admit that I shopped my way through my days and weeks at the factory, whenever I was called in to work. This work paid my bills, but there was never money left over for anything else.

How I resented the miserable hours that I spent at that job! I would take regular trips to Columbus usually every month and buy what I thought I deserved for my stress and suffering. The rebellious part of me wanted to damage myself and prove to God that he had to *give* me a better way of life-- or else I would continue to self-harm. Once again, I wish that I had not felt so entitled! I had so much in my life to be grateful for, but could not manage to keep my focus off of what I did not have.

There were several times during the rocky first year and a half of my business where I actually had a zero balance in my checking account, barely any fuel in my car, and a credit card bill due the next week. A very loyal friend gave me cash during some of those desperate occasions, and guilt overwhelmed me. I was ashamed of my selfishness, and had never quite allowed myself to face the fact that I was taking advantage of and being dishonest with the people in my life who supported my dream and

158

believed in my efforts. It <u>finally</u> occurred to me with shocking displeasure that my mom and my friend deprived themselves of material things because they would rather unselfishly and incredibly generously bail me out of my financial woes. Guilt sickened me, and I realized that I had been avoiding the reality of the situation. I actually *cared* for these people, and how could I go on taking advantage of them??? How could I feel good about wearing my abundance of clothes and shoes, often bought in secret, and allow my mom and my friend to pay my consequences?? Not that either of them were interested in going on shopping sprees similar to mine, but hours and hours of their hard work, representing hours of their actual lives, had gone indirectly into my wardrobe.

Being accountable and facing my guilt was an important step in letting go of my addiction. I don't believe that anyone with an addiction is truly innocent of hurting the people who care about them. To understand that my mom

159

and my friends and my sisters respected me and trusted me was something that I no longer wanted to betray or take for granted. I had developed sneaky habits back when I was a devious and dishonest child and had perfected these methods when I became a self-centered teenager without a conscience. But this was no longer my identity. I was close to God now, had developed a sensitive conscience, and finally had learned to care about someone besides myself. My name changes must have developed in part because I couldn't handle being associated with the person I was before, and I looked for a way to distance myself from the sins of the past months.

I knew that somehow I had to be accountable to the people in my life that I was closest to. I had attempted to involve my mom and my friends in my addiction, sometimes handing over my credit cards to them for safekeeping. But at the rapid rate that I opened and closed new accounts and did balance transfers, this method didn't work out very

160

well. As soon as I had a credit card in my hand again, or got an invoice in the mail, (which had the account number printed right on it) the sneaky side of me couldn't resist outsmarting the part of me that was desperately trying to put an end to my credit card use. All of the little games and tricks I used to prevent myself from buying on credit might work for a month or two, but in the back of my mind I was always looking for an excuse or a way out. I had been putting the responsibility for my credit card use in someone else's hands. While friends and family were glad to try to help me, I needed to fix the problem for myself, for a long-term cure. If I were to become a responsible business owner, I had to get a grip on my personal finances, and would need to be able to trust myself to handle my business' finances. The time had arrived to come face to face with the part of me that was self-destructive and lived for thrill and pleasure. Even if ninety-five percent of me was against the self-destructive

161

nature, why did the unquestionably addicted five percent of me have so much power??

It was the summer of 2010. A very poor summer. But also a summer that was memorable because I began to finally let go and trust God with my finances as well as with my wardrobe. It may sound like the silliest thing in the world to let God have control over my wardrobe, but the truth is, this was the one remaining dark area in my life that took priority over anything else. I had gotten myself into so much debt because of my wardrobe, and it still was far from perfect and _not_ the luxurious collection that I thought I would possess in my thirties. I bravely closed all of my credit cards except for one. Each month I could only spend around $75, as I was close to reaching my credit limit. I _knew_ I was in for a lot of pain, but I had no idea how intense or for how long. I had begun to wonder if my credit card use was preventing my business from growing and preventing me from finding steady part-time work. Superstitious? Perhaps. But I dreaded the factory, the odor of melted plastic there, the loudness, as well as the stale, long, boring and hopeless-feeling work days. That was how all of the employees there seemed to me – colorless and without hope. Sitting all day in the drab, outdated office, just waiting for the president to criticize me for something from the office behind me.

Oddly, there was no work for me all summer at the factory. There was no shopping that I could do, and also no fuel in my car. In my extreme misery, I named myself Sarade, which was, I will now note, the closest any of my other names have ever come to my real name, Sarah. I walked wherever I could, but one day decided to treat myself and drive across town to rent a movie. When I left to drive home from the video store, my car would not start. My heart sank, and devastation temporarily chased away all of my faith in God. It was unbelievable! Just weeks before, I had closed my "emergency" credit cards, and

163

now had a legitimate emergency on my hands. Trusting God with my finances had not gotten me very far—an entire two weeks!?! Though she immediately offered to, I did not want my mom to have to pay for my car repair. Quitting my job for Navare Jewelry was supposed to be my risk, not hers, and I wanted to make absolutely sure that my bills were not her burden. _Really_, what kind of a sign was this?!?

My mind spun, and I wanted a way out of my life – to quit my business, to get a new credit card in order to go on a huge shopping spree, and then file for bankruptcy while I searched again for full-time work. An irresistible escape plan was quickly thrown into place, all before I knew what was wrong with my car. How quick I was to lose my faith in God. And how effortless it was for me to dream of abandoning everything that mattered to me for a shopping spree.

Two days later, I had made no move except to pray and to cry. The call came about my car repair, and, sure enough, it was a major and expensive repair that needed to be done. It was out of my hands, and my mom and her checkbook would step in and save the day. This was **not** okay with me. I remembered having a similar car repair having been done not too long ago, and so I rifled through receipts and found the details. Perhaps there was some kind of warranty if it happened to be the same part for the car. I called to inquire, and was told that it was not the same part at all. One long afternoon later I was finally resigned to accept my unfortunate fate, and I received a miraculous call. Yes, in fact, the part was indeed the same, and it would be covered by a warranty. The car repair ended up costing me nothing. My moods had swung drastically up and down during the course of two days, and, if I had had the available credit I would have drowned my misery in shopping and more debt. I had had no choice but to pray and to go back and forth between faith and devastation and doubt, riding out the storm in my life – and everything had turned out to be fine. God had had my back the whole time, and I was reassured that although I did not deserve it, there was some sort of safety net protecting me from harm. My business and my dream would continue to exist, and I would persist in staying strong against the temptation of my shopping addiction.

Another lesson I learned from the car repair situation, besides trust in God, was to be guided by common sense, *instead of* feelings and moods. As a creative person, and as a female, I *relied* on and valued my feelings. But I had noticed over the years that my moods could change substantially over the course of a single hour, and the powerful destructive moods were capable of demolishing a lot of stability and good that I had spent much effort and discipline accumulating. **Discipline!** I needed to apply discipline to the rebellious and moody areas of my life, or

166

I would continue to destroy myself. I had *always* looked down on common sense as boring and predictable, and as something that was useless in a creative person's life. But I was finally starting to see that wisdom and common sense go hand in hand, and I certainly did aspire to be wise. From this point on, whenever I got an urge to shop (no matter how strong) I had to first slow down my automatic reaction to obey it, and to instead analyze it and think it through, in order determine if there was a genuine need or a legitimate reason behind it. I was already an expert at finding explanations and reasons for my purchases. It was always *my* choice, but didn't I have the freedom to tell my addiction "NO!"?

I had fought my shopping addiction for *so* many years. So why had I never healed or succeeded at getting past a certain point? My life had slowed to a point where I certainly had the time to explore *what* was hiding behind my addiction. How far could I take the pain --- possibly to

167

the point where I experienced it fully and moved on? I had successfully denied myself the acquisition of certain items of clothing in the past. Most memorable was the previous December and the dark blue J Crew coat I had desperately wanted with all of my heart. I had watched the coat obsessively since it had debuted in the fall catalogue. I had spoken of it to friends and family, visited it often online – even going so far on a few occasions as to put the coat into my shopping basket and enter in my information, including credit card number. But I never clicked on the all-important "submit purchase". I now lived my life surrounded by people who didn't care about fashion, most of whom only owned one or two winter coats at the most. I owned more than twenty coats and jackets, and I could hear the disappointment in my best friend's voice when I talked to him about purchasing the blue coat. If one winter coat was good enough for him, not to mention the fact that he had given me money for bills on several occasions, then

168

how dare I consider indulging this selfish desire? I began to force myself to dwell on the expression of pain I would potentially see in the eyes of my friend and my mom, both of whom had protected me from missing credit card payments, if I should continue down this obviously sinful path. Sooner or later it would all catch up with me, my luck would run out, and my chance for a prosperous future would expire.

Chapter 12: The Solution to *Guilt*

All of my life I have lived under the crushing weight of guilt. It had made me miserable and depressed and I now know that a lot of it had to do with my reckless abuse of money. There was a way to alleviate the guilt, which always, inevitably, sent me back into the familiar downward spiral of my shopping addiction. The time to take responsibility for my actions was long overdue. I ***never*** wanted to see the look of disappointment in my mom's or my friend's eyes again. I wanted them to be proud of me, and to demonstrate to them that they had good reason for giving me the benefit of the doubt all along.

Over time I had built a history and a point of reference of occasions when I did not buy a certain item that I coveted. This was proof that I could do it again. To this day, I *still* want that blue J Crew coat, and wish that I had bought it. I even watched it go on sale and somehow had the strength

170

to believe that there would be another coat in the future that I would be able to purchase with cash, and without a guilty conscience. Sometimes these things occur, and many times they don't. So there is never any certainty or magical guarantee that I will get what I want in the future when I deprive myself in the present. But the occasions that this does occur make doing without in the past feel like it was very worthwhile.

Two months after establishing my $75 a month credit card budget, I was offered a seasonal job at a college bookstore. It was minimum wage, and would only last for six weeks, but I was thrilled to be getting a regular paycheck. The job felt like a reward – to finally have the assurance that I would be able to pay my bills for a while. I enjoyed the job, as I'd always loved the educational atmosphere of a college campus. I realize that we can't manipulate God, but I decided way earlier than I ever thought I was ready, that during the first week of September I would take one

171

final shopping trip and then close my last open credit card account. No more monthly budget to use as a safety net. I wanted a permanent job at the bookstore, and really wanted to *never* have to go work at the factory again. Maybe God would reward me with this job if I would take another step to trust Him. Another motivating factor occurred also in late August of that year. I was visiting my best friend in Columbus for the day, and my financial situation was on the brink of collapse. I was an emotional nervous wreck, and I could see that my friend was finally to the point of feeling hesitant about offering to give me money. It was always supposed to be the *last* time, in my mind. I had *never* asked him for money to bail me out of a sticky situation, but on this occasion I was extremely close to begging. I began to wonder if his generosity was enabling me. He always listened to all that I had to say, supported me and believed in my business, and wanted me to succeed. I had a major credit card bill due in a few

172

days. My small bookstore paycheck would not come for another week, I explained to him. I felt so fortunate to have this friend in my life; that he *wanted* to be in my life, despite all of the times that I repeatedly messed up and he had come to my rescue. Not everyone in debt is lucky enough to have such a kindhearted friend who cares so much. I did not want to view this valuable person as an ATM! He ended up offering me the money to pay my bill for what actually was the final time, and I remember being so grateful, having come so close to my first time *ever* not having the means to pay a bill on time. I felt truly that I had hit rock bottom.

Some part of me, the reckless part, had always dared myself to make just one more purchase. Somehow my bills were always paid, so why did I have any reason to think otherwise? I was pushing God to His limit, to find out just how much I could get away with. I didn't see it this way all of the time, but had changed my point of view

173

since I had started my business and had not had a steady income. My too-close-for-comfort experience taught me to let go and to respect authority. I had learned a healthy fear of God and of consequences, and wanted to give everything I had to begin trusting Him and being obedient to His will for me. The constant ups and downs of shopping with credit cards and then being unsure if I could pay my bills were exhausting. I was a nervous wreck, always looking over my shoulder for a "punishment", but the consequences from my years of addiction would be cruel enough. I was fortunate, so fortunate, that my credit history was flawless except for the high debt. I had somehow managed not to ruin my dream for my business. And I was incredibly grateful not to lose the friendship of someone who never believed that I had taken advantage of him. I hadn't intended to, but wasn't the truth of the situation the fact that I had?

My deadline came, and, sure enough, I went on one final small shopping trip and then closed the last emergency credit card. This was the easy part, but it felt as though I had accomplished a major goal. Almost immediately the next day, I was filled with a sense of panic and torturous deprivation. My most used weapon against temptation had to become thought-blocking. Any time ideas of "just one more time" came into my head, I deliberately focused on something else, such as my business or my upcoming birthday. I also focused on being grateful – grateful for all of the nice things I already had, for the fact that creditors were not coming to take away my furniture or my car, and grateful that my debt was not punishable with hard labor or prison time. I didn't *deserve* to get away with all of these crimes against myself and against my mom and my friend. Maybe the immense pain I felt because I was not shopping was a punishment I deserved to experience. Of course it was!! Parents punish their children in order to

175

teach them and help them to become better people, as well as because they love them. God allows pain in our lives and uses it for good – especially, I believe, if it is pain originating from the consequences of self-destructive habits. I did not know to what extent the consequences of my addiction would affect the future, but I did know that I was ready to face the challenges that laid ahead with a new oath that I had never quite had the courage to take. With full force I propelled all of my rebellion and anger into fighting my shopping addiction. When the great pain and agitation and anguish overwhelmed me, I cried, stormed around, prayed, and allowed myself to feel the potent emotions that would hurt but not harm. The pain would serve to initiate my healing from addiction.

September and October 2010 crawled by. They were two absolutely dry month of *no* extra cash, and barely enough money to pay my bills. I received the very good news that the bookstore wanted to keep me as a regular employee,

176

but I would only get about four hours a week. My temptations were heavy, with a dentist appointment and car insurance to pay for, as well as Christmas gifts to purchase. My family and friends assured me that not receiving gifts for Christmas and birthdays was no big deal. But it was a *huge* deal to me, and an even bigger blow to my pride when I had to cut friends out of my shopping list. I planned for the worst – to possibly not be able to buy gifts for my mom, whose birthday also lands on Christmas day. To make matters worse, my cell phone fell out of my purse, along with a bag of pricey makeup, and into a public toilet. Everything was destroyed, and I didn't have the means to replace anything. Was this just part of my trial, or was it a sign that it was useless for me to continue to fight this battle? The harder I had fought over the years to stop shopping, it seemed the stronger my addiction had fought back.

177

I was mentally exhausted from all of the expenses that circulated through my mind. I was worried, felt defeated and weak, and so I submitted to the devastation and allowed my circumstances to lead me where they may. *This* was the solution I finally understood. It didn't actually make sense before – similar to the flexible tube-like Chinese puzzle that traps a finger from both hands in opposite ends…the harder you pull to get them out, the tighter the woven material grasps your fingers. You must gently relax in order to loosen the trap, and then you may carefully slide your fingers free. Letting go, while making a patient and slow attempt to free your fingers. It was either heal or self-destruct at this point. And it was my decision to make.

The depression and voices of failure took me where they may, and then, astonishingly, they left me alone. I trusted God to carry me from this point. I have to admit that the *fear* of depression and deprivation and voices of failure

178

was far worse than actually experiencing the pain they brought with them and then moving on from it. When I let go, then I began to heal. I focused on healing and processing pain, rather than battling the constant urge to shop. It isn't as if I stopped trying or gave up, but realized that I alone did not have the strength to make much improvement.

I made it through the first stage of withdrawal successfully. I had suffered through a dry, lonely, and deprived period of my life that had previously brought out the worst in my addiction, and I couldn't help but compare it to the two and a half empty years of unemployment after my divorce. Some healing had taken place then, but not enough, since I had used shopping to soothe myself. I was encouraged to see how much stronger I had become, or, rather, how much stronger *God* was in *me*. When I had fought myself, I had been divided and weak – easily conquered by my addiction. Instead now I not only prayed

179

for the strength to make it through each new temptation, but understood how to accept my circumstances without my usual rebellion, as God was allowing this deprivation in my life for many good reasons.

November 2010 brought with it all kinds of little surprise monetary rewards – rebates, tithe gifts, extra hours at work, and some jewelry sales here and there. I couldn't believe that I had been *so* worried, but I had ended up able to buy a new cell phone, pay my bills, and had finished off most of my Christmas shopping. I would have liked to have bought better and costlier gifts, but fortunately I had already bought quite a few of them when I'd been using credit cards, and I was grateful to be able to buy the remaining ones, all things considered. So I could reference back to this and see that God would bring money and shopping into my life, but in His own time. I'd lived through a deprived October, only to be rewarded for my patience a month later.

180

Christmas of 2010 arrived, and I braced myself for the over-stimulation of material things, just as I had when my birthday rolled around. Inexplicably to me, an abundance of gifts or new items *always* sets off a fire for <u>more</u>. Maybe I just love material things so much that the excitement within me is contagious. Greed!! Not wanting the bliss to end, I yearn to begin a new hunt for something beautiful or marvelous that will make my life better. I *long* for luxury, and my lifestyle is anything but luxurious at this point. But if I can see progress – lovely new things coming into my life, which often leads to discarding things that remind me of the disappointing life I've led – then I become motivated and encouraged and eager to find out what is next to come. Greed is easily awakened within me, and it was important for me to acknowledge this.

I have noticed within myself a pattern of strong urges or temptations either for a certain item, or for a piece (or several pieces) from a particular retailer about once a

181

month. January's pain was another coat. A plaid trench coat from Anthropologie. It had been on my mind, or in the back of my mind, since I had seen it in the catalogue. I knew it would quickly sell out, and so the craving laid dormant until the over-stimulation of Christmas and then the unbelievable sales of the New Year began.

Anthropologie no longer stocked the coat, but Ebay did --- and it was only $79!! I endured the pain of not buying the coat, but the truth is that the intensity didn't fade. I still crave the coat, and I find myself occasionally browsing online for similar plaid coats, determined and hopeful that one day soon I will have the means to purchase it without guilt.

Amazingly, in January, I was able to buy a pair of shoes and three sweaters using cash. Actual cash!! My friend had given me a gift card for Anthropologie for Christmas, and what a thrill it was to go to my favorite store and purchase a couple of things! As if this were not enough, I

182

was given the good news at the bookstore that, beginning in February, I would be promoted into the part-time visuals and buying position. The promotion at work would mean a raise, and a guaranteed twenty-five hours a week, *not* as a sales associate! My new job had come at the perfect time! I had last worked at the dreaded factory temp job at the beginning of December, and had had a strong intuition that I would never work there again. Two of the factory workers had told me out of nowhere that morning that I didn't look like I fit in there. I took it as a compliment. I had also made several of the workers upset and physically sick with the smell of the fish I had eaten for lunch, and so in more than one way I felt unwelcome there. I had prayed all day long that it would be my last, and at the end of the day, as a sign of deliberate confidence, I took home the seat cushion that I kept in the stockroom. I said "goodbye" twice when I left the building, but no one heard me, and no one replied.

183

Another strong instinct of mine that was right on target –
very similar to the one I'd had about my studio job ending!
And so I ceased to exist in the life of the terrifying factory.
They never scheduled me to work again, and I later found
out that a new full-time secretary had been hired. A true
gut instinct should not be ignored!

With the anticipation of my soon-to-be new job came the
anticipation of all kinds of shopping with my extra
income. I noticed flaws in my wardrobe and definitely
wanted to plan some shoe and pant purchases in order to
dress more professionally. I had an antique fainting couch
that I wanted to have reupholstered, and there was a
reproduction of an inspiring painting that I wanted to own.
Most importantly, my business! I could begin to invest in
advertising more regularly and at the same time pay down
my debt. Maybe I could get a kitten, and visit my friend in
Minneapolis. The list of spending I would do grew with
each fantasy and daydream.

184

The future was bright, and then it wasn't. Just one week before I was due to start training for my new position, I was crushed to learn that the visual merchandiser had decided not to retire, and the store manager had forgotten to tell me when she changed her mind almost a month before. So I had been convinced for weeks that I had a steady part-time job doing something I would enjoy, but it wasn't to be so. Instead, I was cut down to seven hours a week after the rush of the winter semester ended. This was definitely not enough income to pay my bills, with my business generating very few sales and no more work from my temp job. I couldn't imagine anything more unfair! I could not think that there could exist any other thirty-four year old who had wanted and planned and aimed for a successful career as intensely as I had, only to face so many repeated roadblocks and to appear to myself and the rest of the world as a **Nothing!** All along I had told God that I would take the job if it was His will. I hadn't dared to imagine that the job, which would fit as perfectly alongside of my business as it did with my background, would *not* be His will.

Now came a trial as tough as I'd experienced since stopping my credit card use. I was under so much stress financially and infinitely depressed about my situation. Shopping temptations and rebellion swelled up inside of me. Life was *so* unbelievably cruel, and I wanted to fight back against God, and to shop until I felt relief. Or was this part of the test? Did I really trust God, no matter what? What is the worst that could happen if I tried to live through the disappointment I felt? Would insanity take over me if I did not shop? It often felt that way. I had more months ahead of me during which I had to rely on God to meet my needs, rather than a steady paycheck. But wasn't this the mindset I was supposed to have, even with a regular income?

I give a lot of credit to anyone who lives with a person who is battling an addiction. You don't want to be awful and moody and angry and upset, but you <u>are</u>. You <u>must</u> live through the unflattering emotions that threaten to frighten away your family and friends. The pain sometimes seems as intense as if a vital organ is being slowly pulled out of your body. Your instinct is to fight to keep it alive, but you must instead tolerate the pain of the dying organ, and learn to live life without it. I decided logically and on a case by case basis that no one or two or three items was worth caving in to my temptations to shop. I wanted to be healed from my addiction, and I had progressed further than ever before. It was not worth backtracking due to my suddenly unpleasant circumstances. A new coat and five new pairs of shoes was *not* going to solve my problems, but would only serve to make them worse once the guilt set it. I wasn't even sure that I could handle the disappointment I would have

187

in myself if I broke down and used my credit cards. Plus, how would I ever persuade myself to stop again?

I learned firsthand something that is really common sense, but is also something that few of us can usually have the courage to admit. When fighting an addiction it simply does not work, nor is it realistic, to wait for a calm time in your life before you quit. Whether you are drinking, overeating, shopping, or smoking, the stress that defines life will *always* return, and you need to be prepared for battle with a weapon and a coping method *other* than addiction. You will learn who your true friends are when you are in the midst of your battle --- who answers your calls, who has time to listen, even when they don't understand your struggle, and who calls to find out how you *are*, even if you've been in a bad mood the last five times they've spoken with you. I had a great big circle of friends during the prime of my addiction – when I had money to shop and eat out, when I could shop myself into

188

a fun and entertaining mood, and when I generously gave presents. I now have a small circle of loyal friends who actually care about the real me, and who have been endlessly supportive of my battle with addiction, as well as of my business. I am fortunate enough to count on these valuable friends along with my family members.

Chapter 13: The Value of a Dollar

The daunting tasks of pursuing a big dream <u>and</u> kicking an addiction at the same time --- I felt that I wouldn't be able to accomplish one without succeeding at the other. Because I didn't succumb to my shopping temptations after January's major disappointment, I made a major step towards learning obedience to God, and I felt that I definitely had gained new strength and willpower. My tax refund came to save the day in February, and I continued to make careful, well-planned, and responsible cash purchases. With my income well below the poverty level, I put serious thought into even a toothpaste or shower gel purchase. I remember feeling incredibly grateful to be able to buy deodorant on one occasion, and a pack of gum was a treat I bought partially with an assortment of coins I had found while walking. Earning minimum wage, like a teenager with a first job, I really began to understand the value of a dollar. I was ashamed to realize that because I'd

190

stolen money from my parents as a child and a teenager, and then moved to credit card use in college, I'd never allowed myself a chance to appreciate or understand the *true value* of money. As humiliating as it was, my version of poverty was a healthy and beneficial stage for me to start at.

I was **so** poor, and absolutely the poorest of my social group, but knew that in the great scheme of things I was not poor at all. I made deliberate efforts to be glad for things like food and a car and indoor plumbing, as well as privacy and quiet and a bed to sleep in. I felt so very deprived, and shopping cravings continued to harass me. I needed to show God that He could trust me now, during the hard times, so that He could trust me with increased responsibility in what I hoped would be the near future. I knew He was watching every dollar that I spent, as well as every dollar that I gave away. It was astonishing to me to find that although I earned very little money, I had been able to faithfully give away twelve percent of my sales and ten percent of my paychecks and *still* could make ends meet. Since I loved to shop, it was a thrill for me to take this money and spend it on someone else's needs. At the end of each year now when I add up my charitable contributions for tax purposes, I am truly amazed at the grand total that I have parted with. In the past when I had worked full-time, I had always wrongly assumed that I didn't have a high enough income to be able to help someone else. But I'd always heard from people who gave away ten percent of their income to someone less fortunate, that no matter how it looked like it would turn out to be next to impossible to do, their financial situations actually became less stressful by the act of giving. I had been brave and finally attempted this in my own life because I wanted God to prosper my business and I believe that by *giving*, I started to heal my addiction. It is so rewarding to look back and see the gradual – very

192

gradual slowing of shopping with credit cards, and the courage that had built up in increments which enabled me to call the companies and close my cards and lower my credit limits one at a time. It was a combination of tiny steps that led to my healing, as well as a focus on victories I had when I didn't succumb to a certain clothing temptation. I definitely had an abundance of failures to look back on, but it would only discourage my progress to dwell on those memories.

By February 2011, I was a full six months into my life without credit cards. It was another tough month when I felt as if God was really turning up the heat on me, to burn away my addiction. I was pleased to be able to acquire a new credit card in order to do a zero percent interest balance transfer from another of my credit cards that had been charging interest on the balance. I was simply dying to allow myself my habitual traditional one purchase to break in my new card. Because I had sold my small black

193

Prada bag to pay bills, I had in mind a splurge on a new black handbag, since whose wardrobe could be considered complete without one? Instead, I forged ahead, determined to develop new and healthy habits and traditions, and to be grateful for the handbags I already possessed. I had *never* felt so positive that I was moving in the right direction with my life, despite the fact that my business was slow, and my tiny bookstore paychecks went automatically to pay routine credit card bills. I wasn't willing to exchange that invaluable and hard-to-come-by positive feeling for guilt. A black handbag at that point would have meant my certain downfall. I could convince myself that the future held for me an even better black handbag than one I could purchase at this point in time. I also held onto a lingering fear of being called back into the factory if I were to succumb to my addiction again. The dull torture chamber of a workplace that represented a trap and a failure and a place where dreams could not exist. I was sure that God was pleased with my progress, and I did not want to risk His displeasure and a possible punishment for relapse. Whether it was God or my own imagination that created this fear, I believe it was healthy, and it certainly was effective.

It was bitterly difficult to be on such a different path in life from my friends. I spoke often to them of my addiction and of my decision to start writing this book, but addiction is something that seems to be impossible to understand unless you have experienced it for yourself. If I searched in my small city, I knew I would find overeaters anonymous and alcoholics anonymous meetings, but mine was a lonely path. This shopping addiction just wasn't a practical addiction that I could very easily find a local support group to attend for help. There was no special recognition or pat on the back for making it one month, six months, or a year without using my credit cards. I found myself making small announcements to coworkers, family, and friends, whenever I had made it through another month of success. It felt like such an accomplishment, and I knew the significance of it, but it was difficult to explain, especially to anyone who didn't like to shop. Living with a shopping addiction, I was sort of in the same boat as someone who overeats. You are not able to declare that you will never eat or shop again. You must instead relearn the behavior, but with difficult-to-learn moderation.

My personality tends to be all or none, and I know that I share this with a great percentage of not only addicts but passionate people in general. Especially when it comes to food and shopping! Fortunately my consistent efforts to be healthy, as well as my love of fashion, aid me in limiting my food intake. Shopping with credit cards is like eating with a no-limits metabolism. Just like many overweight people have lost the ability to feel satiated or a loss of appetite from being full, I had somewhere along the line lost the ability to determine when I had enough of something, like shoes or coats. An example of one of my problem areas is bras and panties – in matching sets or as separates. I could find so many beautiful pieces and acquired them faster than they wore out. One day I counted what I had, just out of curiosity. A friend who worked for Victoria's Secret had nowhere nearly as many as I had, and, after I questioned a few other friends, it was plain to see that the size of my collection had grown large enough. I made a reasonable decision right then that I had *plenty*. After this, the rule was that I could only go out in search of new bras or panties if there was truly a need; that is if I had thrown away some that had worn out or no longer fit properly. In this way, I learned to get the value out of something I had paid for. It gave me a sense of peace, at least in one area of my wardrobe. This was a frustrating route for me, especially whenever a new Victoria's Secret catalogue came in the mail, or one of their Semi-Annual sales started, but it turned out to be

197

quite effective. I began to apply this method to my eye shadows and lip glosses, as well as my socks and tights. I did not want my purchases to be wasteful, nor did I want any part of my wardrobe to be outdated.

I have, due mainly to budget restraints, and now also thankfully due to common sense, made every attempt not to shop for fun and entertainment, but to go out seeking certain items that I have concluded beforehand that my wardrobe is lacking. I have often discovered that on many occasions now when I add a new piece of clothing to my wardrobe, I am able to clearly notice an older piece or two that are outdated or are no longer my style, and remove these from my wardrobe. My wardrobe as well as my sense of style have absolutely improved since I have put God in charge. I still have fun and am entertained when I shop, but I no longer permit myself to go out and shop purely for the sake of entertainment or because I am bored or sad or lonely or frustrated. I am relieved to realize that

198

my days of ridiculous purchases such as Hello Kitty trinkets and brightly colored ill-fitting tops from Target's girls' department have come to an end! If it is cheap or too trendy or ill-fitting in the least, it likely does not have a place in my well-edited wardrobe.

March 2011 was a month of priorities. While I had a lovely chunk of money from my tax refund still sitting in my bank account, a pair of irresistible grey riding boots was calling my name. I wisely, instead, invested in a month-long online ad space for my business. I felt that I needed to make another motion to prove that my business took priority over fashion. Frustratingly, I had zero resulting sales, and desperately wanted revenge for the heartbreak I felt! Not only did I want to break my 6-month record of no credit card use by purchasing the grey boots, but I also had my eye on the most mouthwateringly beautiful black lace and deep blue blouse at FreePeople.com. I was certain that if I held off from

199

buying it, God would understand how much I wanted this piece, how well it would fit into my wardrobe, and I hoped that He would reward me for waiting on *Him* to provide a way to buy it.

Days and weeks passed, and money *did* come into my life, but so did bills. I always had a choice – to postpone a bill payment and risk not paying it in order to acquire the blouse, or to take the deliberate responsible action of paying bills first in order to protect my credit and the future of my business. My wardrobe was the ultimate sacrifice, finally, and I had to hourly and daily turn control of it back over to God. I periodically checked my gorgeous blouse online and watched with a mixed sense of panic and calm as first there were two, then one, and then none left in my size. I was dying to shop, dizzy with cravings, and actually felt near collapse. I exercised to relieve my frustration, but inside I was screaming over and over.

200

During this battle over the Free People blouse, I felt as if I was staring my addiction directly in its evil eyes. I was involved in a very real physical and mental battle. I wanted to run into the soothing and familiar arms of my shopping addiction and forget about the failure that my life was! My stagnant business made me miserable; and shopping would help to ease the pain. Screams and anguish and the poison of my addiction flailed about inside of me, and I prayed desperately for God to use that pain for good, even as I cried. The pain was overwhelming, but I had begun to notice that in everyday life I handled stress more maturely, panicked less often, and felt less intense anxiety as a result of life in general. Some part of me still expected myself to give up the battle, just as I always had before. Another superior new part of me understood that this time was different – that I <u>was</u> slowly healing from my addiction. My addiction had never been more visible to me and available to battle than it was when I was feeling

201

miserable and deprived. I forced my anger against my addiction, and away from its usual path against God and then inevitably myself.

In early April the coveted Free People blouse went on sale. I felt myself scrambling like an addict to come up with some way, any way possible, to buy the shirt in the next size up. I planned to have it altered. I had the cash to get it – the choice was mine - but I legitimately needed other things like sunscreen and face wash. Buying the blouse would have caused me to have a zero balance in my checking account, and *still* have a list of basic items I needed for day-to-day life. In my heart, I knew what the correct decision was, but I appreciated having the freedom to make the choice for myself. After all, I had only created unhappiness for myself in the past by allowing myself to buy whatever I wanted. I had nothing to lose by sticking with God's plan. I had a glimmer of hope and faith that obedience and common sense might soon bring prosperity into my life.

It was around this same time that it occurred to me to really look at luxury goods in a different way than I ever had before. I began to feel disgusted when I read stories in magazines or saw features on television, where money has clearly been wasted on items that could have been luxurious without costing as much as the average person earns in a year's time. So many people in the world live in poverty, and I am rightfully ashamed of all of the money and credit I threw away on meaningless junk. Just how extravagant do our homes and our cars and our wardrobes need to be? At a certain point, an overly expensive item is a statement to everyone else that you are superior to them.

Every dollar in my bank account, I finally realized, is a gift from God, even if I personally worked hard to earn it. The ability to work, as well as the job, is a gift from God that I have learned not to take for granted. I love fashion and appreciate fine quality as much as, if not more than, anyone I know, but at a certain price point a luxury price tag is more about ego than need or function. *No one* needs a gold toilet seat. Why have a $500,000 engagement ring, when you can have an equally beautiful ring that costs so much less? There would be money left over for additional jewelry, with loads of money left over to help someone whose life isn't quite as prosperous. I have to ask myself: Is it even ethical to wear something valuable enough that someone would take your life for it?

I noticed that when I own and/or wear an item that costs too much, every waking hour becomes more about focusing on protecting that item than it does about living my actual life. The safety and wellbeing of the item somehow has more importance than my own comfort, just based on its value. Some of my favorite jewelry is vintage, and a lot of my clothing came from thrift stores and cost me less than $10 apiece. As for shoes, handbags, and sunglasses .... styles change! I seldom realize it worth my while to spend more than I can afford on pieces that wear out or that will inevitably look outdated in a few years. I can plan to spend more on classic pieces, but even classic styles change. As items in my wardrobe wear out, I can feel at ease to go out shopping in search of replacements, based on need, and it is refreshingly rewarding and guilt-free!

I am not the girl anymore who wishes to own a hundred handbags....but I'd be okay with a number in the low double digits! I have fewer than ten nice handbags right now that I switch back and forth between, and it feels like so much less of a hassle not to change my handbag with every outfit. I never understood this before now, but my material things were really weighing me down. The last few years of little to no income has forced me to let go of things I had previously clung to --- an Armani watch, a

Prada handbag, a Marc Jacobs jacket, and my knight's helmet and German sword. All things I splurged on and believed that I'd have forever. But when times got tough and I needed to pay bills, my fondness for these things faded. It was easier than I expected to sell off my gold jewelry, when now I think it was just the idea of it being gold jewelry that made me want to keep it. It turns out, I would rather have my unique vintage jewelry, which is definitely more my style, and I absolutely don't miss my "status" items at all! I won't deny the fact that there are many new status items that I lust after, but for now, they will have to wait. And any future high ticket item that I do buy will be a carefully planned investment.

Jewelry, shoes, cars, multiple homes, high-priced designer clothing and overly expensive beauty products--- we only live so long, so if the money we spend on things, justified only a small percentage or up to a certain point by quality, is above a certain amount, then we are certainly choosing

206

the temporary material things of this world over human lives. How many minimum wage dollars does it take to buy a pair of Louboutin's? And how many people throughout the world are not even fortunate enough to earn as much as our United State minimum wage? It wasn't until I was forced to work again for minimum wage that I pondered this, and started to weigh the price tag of every purchase against the hours of my life that were needed to pay for it. There is unlimited luxury in this world, but there is also unlimited poverty and suffering and I am glad and grateful to realize *before* I am a success what an absolute crime it is to turn your back on all of this *need* for excessive and pointless shopping, ridiculously high quality clothing worn only a few times, and very expensive fine jewelry. These costly items proclaim to most of the world: "*I am superior to you and these frivolous things are worth more to me than your comfort, health, suffering, or life*".

Chapter 14: Starving the Addiction

In May 2011 I had two cavities that needed to be filled, with no dental insurance, and no way to pay for the bill. My Mom offered to help me, and I turned her down, wanting to experience for myself the reality of the situation. My dentist had a gradual payment plan, and I could pay as little as $10 a month on my almost $300 bill. My intent was to live within my means, but the tiny paychecks from the bookstore were barely covering my regular monthly bills. Deprivation-wise, I felt that I had just about reached my limit long ago. It seemed to me that my entire summer wardrobe was worn out, but anytime I had extra money, I forced myself to do the responsible thing and paid on my dentist bill. For someone who is fashion obsessed, facing the fact that you are unable to update your worn-out wardrobe is a pretty intense dose of pain. I came dangerously close to making a credit card purchase, and my addiction was like a writhing monster inside of me. Killing my addiction by not feeding it was anguish! I was starving for material things!!

I began to see a little bit of a pattern in my life in regards to my periods of trials and deprivation. Just when things seemed like they couldn't get any worse every month or two – when bills piled up and I was running low on everything from gluten-free bread to shampoo and couldn't afford to replace anything --- I would reach what felt like a lowest point, where I could barely, just barely, handle not making a purchase. I would find myself getting a ridiculous thrill from a carefully planned purchase of toothpaste or dental floss, and I can appreciate this because it brought me to the point of finally being *grateful*. I would breathe a huge sigh of contented relief whenever I could replenish some of my day-to-day necessities as the result of a jewelry sale or surprise extra hours at the bookstore. I had been doing online surveys for many months to earn extra money, and was suddenly able to

209

cash in on some of these during the summer. A friend gave me tips on how to use EBay, and so a lot of my clothing that no longer suited me brought in little bits of extra income. The best thing of all during the middle of what looked like promised to be a very poor summer was a sudden gift of five boxes full of vintage jewelry and buttons. Any time I was ready to just give up on my business as a failure, God somehow surprised me and brought encouragement in the form of supplies or sales. I wasn't able to use much of the five boxes of jewelry and buttons to create new pieces with, but I was able to either sell it on EBay, or trade and sell some of it to one of my regular jewelry suppliers. God blessed me with enough money to pay off my dentist bill, buy a few summer clothes, and to pay other regular bills while I scraped by on five hours a week at the bookstore!

Slowly, ever so slowly, God caused my income to grow. Summer progressed, and I came closer to the triumphant one full year without credit card use. In my mind, making it an entire year had huge significance. The manager at the bookstore had promised me more hours – fifteen to twenty a week starting in the fall, and I had plans to establish a more professional website apart from Etsy if I could afford the monthly fee. I was impatient, but continued to find more clothing at thrift stores to sell on EBay. I continued to work on this book, and promoted my business in any way I could think of. I mailed out packages of free jewelry to celebrities and fashion bloggers, and saw my sales increase a little from what they had been during the previous two summers. I kept my eye on my goals --- my business, as well as getting out of debt, and watched the total amount I owed to creditors creep down one minimum payment at a time.

Fall semester started at the bookstore, and I had an abundance of hours for several weeks. After bills were paid, I had some extra money left over for a few clothes

I'd been needing. I needed new boxes for my jewelry business, and made that a priority. My minimum wage paychecks were still pretty small, and I had to carefully consider where I would spend each dollar. Would I invest in new business cards and advertising, start shopping away at the long list of Christmas and birthday gifts to be bought before the end of the year, or allow myself to hunt for the pants and shorts that my wardrobe lacked? I ended up sending a little of the money in each direction, trying my best to wisely distribute my resources.

On the day before the one-year anniversary of no credit card use, I went with a friend to the local outlet mall. I actually trembled with anxiety on the morning before the trip, and considered backing out. The outlet malls had been a favorite place for dozens of my previous shopping binges. I faced the challenge prepared with coupons and a $50 gift card earned from completing online surveys. I boldly turned away from a few beautiful pieces of clothing

212

that were just not practical in my life, with only a little regret. I acquired some new tops, and left the outlet mall with money in my bank account – probably for the first time ever. I felt victorious!!!

For some reason, I didn't find the new pants and shorts that I had planned to buy. In the past this would have set me into an unsatisfied frame of mind, and I would have felt compelled to shop and spend until I finally found what I was looking for, as well as everything else in between. I was a bit disappointed, but couldn't believe the marvelous additions I had made to my wardrobe without the use of credit cards. I supposed that when the timing was right, God would allow new pants and shorts into my life, but He was in charge of my wardrobe, and I must confess that it had never looked better!

It was still 2011, but September 5, 2011 was a new year for me. Partially as a reward for making it through an

213

entire year, and partially out of curiosity, I had decided to allow myself a single purchase on a credit card. My one stipulation was that this item would be something on my needs list. Since I had sold my small and impractical black Prada handbag the year before, I decided that instead of a coat, a new black handbag would be the most reasonable item to buy. I shopped around and found one I liked for a not-outrageous price. Because I spent less that I'd originally planned to on the handbag, immediately all kinds of possibilities for additional credit card purchases occurred to me. Did I want to open the door to this temptation any further than I already had?

In the emptiness that was my life at that time – I *felt* my addiction – and it was weaker and smaller than it had ever been. It was easier than I thought it would be to say "No!" to additional purchases, not wanting to make a mockery out of my efforts for the past year. Obeying a previously made wise decision was something I had really

214

learned to do, inside and out, during the past challenging year. And besides, hadn't God just given me all kinds of surprise new pieces of clothing during the last month? I just had to trust that the grey riding boots and the olive green snow boots that represented my current cravings would be permitted into my life, but in God's perfect timing. My greed would always be waiting, ready to take advantage of me. I had set myself back, debt-wise, by about a month, with the purchase of my handbag, and I braced myself for strong temptation on the days that followed.

Guilt from my single credit card purchase never came, but a burning desire for more and more material things followed. I could not stop thinking of shopping!! I suddenly had extra money coming in from surveys and EBay, and had had larger paychecks for a few weeks from the busy month at the bookstore. There were so many beautiful fall clothes I wanted to buy, but I intentionally

215

focused my thoughts on my business, bills, Christmas shopping, and an upcoming dentist appointment. My birthday was approaching, and I knew that the overstimulation of so many new purchases, along with gifts I would receive, would endanger my discipline. I had made three trips to Columbus during September, each involving some shopping. There was also a trip to a Dayton mall with my mom, and a thrilling surprise sale at the Gap, for which I had another $50 survey gift card. I acquired so many fabulous new things, including the shorts I had been seeking since spring, but I could only dream of MORE!

These familiar and powerful feelings of greed frightened me. I entered October 2011 spoiled and uncertain of convincing reasons anymore of why I should not use my credit cards now and then. I had been so certain that my year of strictly using cash had healed me for good. Why, then, was I craving a major online binge?? I should have been unselfishly concentrating on Christmas shopping, but sweaters and coats from the fall Boden catalogue circulated in my mind constantly. I was so incredibly tempted to order two pairs of pants from Express on my credit card. After all, they were needs, weren't they? I should be responsible enough by now to decide when something could be charged onto a credit card. I questioned the boundaries that I had set for myself. Was living within my tiny means so essential anymore, now that I knew that I could make it through an entire year using just cash?

I postponed, day after day, any decisions regarding the use of my credit cards. I felt deprived, but was this feeling the true reality, since I had just bought so many new things the month before? How could I go from feeling overindulged to feeling deprived in just a matter of days or weeks? I allowed myself to seriously consider a pants purchase or a plaid coat purchase on my credit cards. When I slowed

217

down my mind enough to think through the situation, to imagine the credit card purchase, the fact that I did indeed have the freedom to make my own choice, it no longer seemed like such a life or death case. The pants were not an emergency. Yes, I loved the plaid coat at Boden, but I didn't really care for the buttons. Shouldn't I hold out for something that was perfect? If, in a few weeks, all of my remaining pants were so worn out that I absolutely had no other option than to use my credit card to buy new pants, this would be considered a true emergency. Other than that, I felt okay about letting go of my plans for any type of immediate purchase. What would be the point? If I began to use my credit card for pants or a coat, how long would I wait before using it again? I had to establish clear and sensible goals for myself, based on common sense; otherwise I would go on another wasteful shopping binge as soon as I had a depressing or stressful day.

218

I calculated that there was around $800 worth of merchandise that I was craving and felt that I needed, and I knew from years of experience that as soon as I acquired these things, I would inevitably find more that I couldn't live without. This was the strongest that my shopping temptations had been for a long time, and I knew that I was in the midst of yet another trial or test. Yes, I had the job at the bookstore, but there was still always the danger of having to go back to work at the factory for some reason or another. Also, with the third year of my business approaching, it was the time to decide whether or not to continue pursuing it, or to partially give up and seek full-time work again. I didn't know how I would face giving up on my dream, and I didn't want to jeopardize my business by displeasing God and getting into more debt. It was so gratifying to finally have regular paychecks and to be able to pay my bills without question. But I had doubts as to if God even cared anymore about my credit card use.

Spending on my credit card would give me immediate and temporary gratification, but this was fleeting, and the gratification would quickly be replaced by a sense of guilt and isolation from God. I was working on the next important step in my business – establishing a new website independent from Etsy, and this was certainly not the time to alienate myself from God. I felt my addiction in motion, but I could conquer it one hour at a time with clear reasoning and common sense, so long as I wasn't afraid to face reality. My reality, the fear of my debt, the frustration over my business, and the confusion regarding my career in general, would remain the same if I were to indulge in my addiction. October led to November and I was drowning in misery. Dwelling on all of the privileges in life that the people around me had – the things that I longed for – like vacations and my own computer and a house and my own cat. I felt so ambitious, but none of the efforts I made towards my business seemed to have much impact.

Chapter 15: Falling Again

Gradually over the next three years, I am ashamed to admit that I began using a credit card occasionally. At first, just to see how it felt. A small promotion at the bookstore prompted me to finally get my own kitten, and she had two expensive vet visits within the first few months. Around the same time, my car's transmission went out, devouring most of my tax refund money, and I began to doubt the protection from God that I had believed to be a condition of me not using my credit cards. Whose rule was it that God was not going to allow any financial emergencies into my life if I obediently abstained from credit card use? My rule, it was, and my world came crashing down around me as my computer died and I had another emergency car repair, with no other way to pay for these things than with credit. What exactly was going on? These emergencies crushed me to the point of near hopelessness. Over the years my debt had diminished by about a third with just the minimum payments I had been making, but now my debt started to creep back up as I recklessly purchased a new phone and satisfied other occasional cravings for shoes, clothing, and cosmetics.

Though I had closed all of my credit cards years ago, I had gradually opened new accounts in order to do balance transfers onto 0% interest rate cards. Because I had grown to trust myself, I eventually ended up with all available and open accounts. This really did work for me for a while, as I still didn't often make purchases with this forbidden payment method. I still had the fear lingering in the back of my mind that God would send me to work at the factory again if I didn't keep my urges under control.

Fast-forward to October of 2014. My beloved store manager at the bookstore retired, and I miraculously found slightly higher paying work as a retail reset merchandiser one week after he left. My new job would start as temporary, but would be forty hours a week and would also be one step closer to the visual merchandising job that I knew that I was destined for. Beginning in January, the recruiter told me, I would become a permanent employee! I had only ever gotten around 25 hours per week at the bookstore, and so I imagined the rapid rate at which my debt would shrink once I earned those larger paychecks.

Well, more bad news for me in my long line of jobs leading up to the perfect career. This job was not only just a dead-end job working at a local grocery store, but it was rough and dirty, and wasn't anywhere near the forty hours I had been promised. It was also nothing very comparable to visual merchandising, with the exception of the job title. Immediately I was horrified, but trapped. And then the holidays came and I had an entire month of no work, as the grocery store didn't want us doing resets in the stores while they were much busier. I tried to focus on my business, but months had started to go by without jewelry

224

sales. During tax season I realized how much better I did by selling thrift store clothing on EBay, and finally made the painful decision to let my little business go. I was spread too thin, and needed to put my focus on finding full-time, professional work.

As my despair with my job grew, so did my credit card usage. I had given my business to God as the ultimate sacrifice, and He didn't cause it to grow. So for the first time in my life I felt completely lost and without the anchor that the great dream of my business had been. As for the fear of working in the factory, the job as a retail reset merchandiser was actually *worse* than that environment had been, and so I no longer had the fear to steel me against shopping urges. Much of my cherished wardrobe was too nice to wear at my dirty workplace. I also lost touch with jewelry altogether, as my vintage accessories would have been damaged while I worked.

225

During my year as a retail reset merchandiser, I had several interviews for visual merchandising positions at Macy's. My interviews were encouraging, and I began to believe that I was destined to work at Macy's. In anticipation of my new role, I began to charge new items of black clothing to my Macy's charge card, as Macy's employee dress code is all black. I didn't have the new job yet, and so I didn't go nearly as overboard as I had when I'd gotten the job at Anthropologie. I wisely stopped short of purchasing any black shoes, as a little voice in the back of my mind reminded me that I should wait until I was hired.

Having already spent much of a first paycheck from Macy's that I hadn't yet received, I also realized that working at the grocery store had taught me to wear repeats of my clothing and to feel okay about it. For once in my career, every day was not about the outfit I had put

226

together or debuting a new piece. And if I did have a new piece of clothing to wear, it had most likely come from a thrift store.

On the 4th of July 2015, I received the final and devastating news by email that I did not get the visual merchandising position at Macy's. The job would not have paid well, but it would have been a foot in the door for what I imagined to be the ideal career for me, aside from my business. I had loved most of my work at the photo studio, and visual merchandising would be another active and creative alternative. Alas, I was nearing 40, and perhaps it was time for an extremely sensible and serious evaluation of my career path. Once again, in a job that made me perhaps the most miserable I had ever been, shopping was the one thing that I had to look forward to. But throughout the summer my hours had dwindled to the point that it was all I could do to pay my bills. Without

227

my credit cards, there would be no shopping. I was grateful for my tiny EBay business, but shopping for additional items to sell also became an impossibility as my income shrank. No matter how many jobs I applied for, I could not seem to find full-time work. And fulfilling work was but a dream, I supposed.

I came to a point where I made a weekly and sometimes bi-weekly purchase with a credit card. Much improved from years ago, but still, obviously, a problem. I finally came up with the courage and determination to close all of my credit cards. I felt a little panicked, at first, but, miraculously, not being able to shop did not cause the painful withdrawal in me that it once had. Though I had taken some steps backwards in paying off my debt and indulging my addiction, I had obviously learned some things! I was no longer such a slave to shopping, and I *could* handle some of life's pain without acquiring more material things. I had to credit God for gradually and permanently changing me, and I had to believe that living so close to family was providing me with something I needed that money couldn't buy. As my readers can surmise, healing from my shopping addiction has been a long and tedious process. It is *not* going to happen overnight, and, just as with any type of addiction, you are never going to be completely healed. I have learned that it is important to monitor my shopping-related activities, as well as to be especially on guard during emotional times of my life, whether happy or sad.

One month before my 40th birthday, I postponed the plans I had made to return to school to study human resources, and accepted a job at a non-profit organization. The job has nothing to do with either of my degrees or my past work experience, and the pay is low. But there are many positives! There is room to grow and to be promoted, and the entire company is immersed in a culture of kindness.

It is terrific to dress professionally again, and to rediscover the clothing and jewelry that had been left behind for the past year.

When I first began writing this book, I imagined that it would be a journey of complete healing; exchanging my shopping addiction for a successful business. God had other plans in mind for my career, and the journey is far from being over. I will never consider the years I spent working on my business as a waste, as that time taught me so much about sacrifice, and about giving my all to something that was extremely important to me. It was vital for me to realize that I had things in my life that were more important than my wardrobe. The tiny income that I earned during these years healed my addiction substantially by teaching me that I could live without constant new things, and taught me the true value of a dollar.

I realize that my shopping addiction is not cured. It seemed impossible to finish this book unless it was cured and until I had figured out all of the answers. Shopping in moderation will always be an issue for me, and the consequence is that I will spend many years paying off the debts that I have incurred. But that's okay. I am making progress. I was waiting for a happy ending, i.e., success in my career or my business before I concluded this book. And recently I realized that I was postponing happiness, and that I had never given myself permission to be content, mainly because I did not have a real career. I spent so many hours searching for happiness in stores and shopping malls. Meanwhile, life has been passing me by as I searched for "perfect". And attempted to attain a perfect wardrobe by living beyond my means. Most of the time now I realize that credit card use is not worth it, as I am once again starting to see my debt diminish.

I need to be okay with where I am now and with the mistakes that I know will be unavoidable in the future. Far from being negative, I think this approach allows me to be comfortable with *me* in uncomfortable situations, therefore there will not be so many occasions when I need to "become" someone else by purchasing the wardrobe of someone who I cannot afford to be. The rapid rate at which I replace my wardrobe and purchase new pieces has slowed during the past decade. I can observe this in spite of my frequent credit card use during the past year.

This has been my path as a shopping addict whose shopping sprees were closely intertwined with frustrating attempts to build a career and to find happiness. This has been a journey, which is far from over, and thus far I have finally developed the courage just to be Sarah, and not to assume all of the other dozen or so identities of the characters I created who not only dressed better than I

232

could afford to, but had better lives than me. My over-spending was all about avoiding reality and escaping the pain that I have now found it necessary to accept in order to live the life that I was meant to live.

Philippians 4:12 is my new goal for the future, as well as a commitment to trust God with my career path and my wardrobe.

I know what it is to be in need, and I know what it is to have plenty. I have learned the secret of being content in any and every situation, whether well fed or hungry, whether living in plenty or want.

Printed in Great Britain
by Amazon